The Cheat Code to Life

Vishnu Saraf is an entrepreneur-turned-author and content creator whose story is one of extraordinary resilience and reinvention. An alumnus of SRCC and IIM Ahmedabad, he began his career at McKinsey & Company and Deutsche Bank before founding a nutrition start-up valued at over ₹150 crore, helping more than 2 lakh people transform their health.

After the pandemic and a series of personal crises that saw him lose everything he had built, Vishnu rebuilt his life from scratch. Today, he inspires millions with his philosophy: 'Bounce Forward'.

Recognised as one of the Top 101 Global Healthcare Leaders by the World Health and Wellness Congress, Vishnu now uses his voice and content to help people rise stronger from any setback.

Advance Praise for *The Cheat Code to Life*

'From a small-town boy to an IIM-A grad who lost everything and rebuilt his life, Vishnu shares raw, relatable lessons on happiness, money, relationships and resilience. If you've ever felt you were meant for more, this is your sign to begin.'

Ankur Warikoo, Entrepreneur and Influencer

'This book offers something rare—real-life wisdom, shared with heart, humour and humility. A must-read for anyone seeking clarity in today's noisy world.'

V.V.S. Laxman, Cricketer

'Beyond the balance sheets and PowerPoints lies the crucial domain of personal mastery. This book provides a roadmap for cultivating the essential life skills that empower us to lead with purpose and impact. A timely reminder that investing in ourselves is the greatest investment we can make. I recommend it.'

Ravi Venkatesan, former Chairman, Microsoft India

'This isn't just a book—it's a personal workshop packed into pages. Vishnu writes from the heart, with honesty and warmth that's rare. His stories are real, his lessons actionable and his style refreshingly simple. You don't just read this book—you reflect, feel and grow with it. A powerful companion for anyone seeking clarity, courage and change.'

Anurag Kedia, Founder, Pilgrim Cosmetics

The Cheat Code to Life

The Real-World Guide to Living Smarter, Healthier & Happier

Vishnu Saraf

Published by Westland Books, a division of Nasadiya Technologies Private Limited, in 2026

No. 269/2B, First Floor, 'Irai Arul', Vimalraj Street, Nethaji Nagar, Alapakkam Main Road, Maduravoyal, Chennai 600095

Westland and the Westland logo are the trademarks of Nasadiya Technologies Private Limited, or its affiliates.

ISBN: 9789371977531

10 9 8 7 6 5 4 3 2 1

Typeset by Mukul

Printed at Thomson Press (India) Ltd

For every soul that believes a better life is possible
and is willing to work for it.

And to my father, the first hero I ever knew,
and the quiet strength behind every step I take.

Contents

Section 2
SUCCESS

Section 3
MONEY

Section 4
RELATIONSHIPS

Section 5
HEALTH

Your Map to This Book

I. Happiness Code

J: Jump Back *(Building Resilience)*
O: Open Outlook *(Shifting Mindset and Emotional Lens)*
Y: Your Love *(Love that Heals)*

II. Success Code

A: Aim *(Set Your Compass for Success)*
C: Cultivate *(Shape Your Inner Game)*
E: Execute *(Move Fast and Smart)*

III. Money Code

M: Mindset *(How You Think About Money)*
A: Awareness *(Seeing Money Clearly)*
P: Prosperity (*Building and Living Wealth)*

VI. Relationship Code

B: Build Trust *(Everyday Relationships)*
A: Appreciate Differences *(Beginning of Romantic Relationships)*
E: Evolve Together *(Deepening Romantic Relationships)*

V. Health Code

F: Fuel First *(Eat Smarter. Eat Better)*
I: Inside Science *(Know What Your Body Really Needs)*
T: Train Smart *(Move Better, Not Just More)*
T: Transform *(Where Habits Turn into Health)*

Introduction: You are Meant for More—Now Prove It

'Formal education will make you a living; self-education will make you a fortune.'

—Jim Rohn

(... and probably every student who's ever Googled 'how to get rich without math')

Scene 1

A skinny fifteen-year-old kid sat in one corner of a classroom in a small town in Bihar. He had good marks but zero confidence. His permanent spot was the corner seat in the last row. He sat quietly, his eyes peering at the table. He wanted to raise his hand but didn't. The words didn't come easily to him—not in English.

He worried that people would laugh. He feared proving his worst suspicion: that he wasn't good enough. So, he did what most of us do when we're scared. He blended in. He nodded silently. He pretended he didn't want more. But deep down, he was lonely. Frustrated. Miserable.

Scene 2

Ten years later. Same kid. Different universe.

He had now graduated from the University of Delhi's prestigious Shriram College of Commerce. Then IIM Ahmedabad. He had published a book with one of the world's top publishers. He had built a start-up of his own.

Confidence? Check. Happiness? Real. Clarity? Work in progress. Accent? Still desi. But he didn't give a damn. What changed? No overnight miracle. No 5 a.m. routine. Just one stubborn thought: *I will grow every single day.*

If that version of him—scared, confused, playing small—could rewrite his script, why not you?

This Book Is for Anyone Who's Done Pretending

Maybe you're in your own Scene 1. Stuck. Doubting. Feeling left behind. This book is for the version of you that's done surviving and is ready to build. Not by luck. Not by privilege. By mindset. With grit. With small brave steps.

I'm not writing this as an expert. I'm writing this as that awkward fifteen-year-old who stumbled, fell and kept getting back up, over and over. This is for anyone who has ever looked in the mirror and thought: *I'm meant for more*. And believed it.

This book is for you if you've ever wondered why most self-help books read like sedatives. Why haven't books evolved when fashion and film have? Why are we still writing for twenty-five-year-olds like they were born in the 1960s? And why the hell do we need 300 pages just to say one thing?

If this book had a Tinder bio, it would say: 'Short. Fun. Emotionally available. Will not ghost you after page 10.'

Don't treat this book like a Bible. Or me like a baba in sneakers. Drop the expert; awaken the doer in you. Treat every idea here as a hypothesis, not gospel. Try it. Test it. And if it doesn't work for you, toss it and move on. Try something new.

This Book Will Teach What Schools Forgot

Do you know that only one in four graduates end up working in their field of study? But all four have to learn how to deal with anxiety at 2 a.m. Schools teach us a lot of things we never use. They teach us about chlorophyll. But not how to say 'no' without guilt.

Neither do they teach us how to:

- Stay sane when shit hits the fan
- Build wealth without selling your soul (or your sleep)
- Love without losing yourself
- Live a disease-free life (without karela juice)

Some might say this stuff can't be taught. That's bullshit. These are skills, not divine blessings. And yes, you can (and should) learn them.

Read on. Your excuses just ran out.

Turns Out My Name Was a Self-Help Blueprint

And since this book is about filling missing gaps, I found inspiration hiding in plain sight: my own name.

Names carry weight. Mine—Vishnu—has always been a quiet dare: live up to it. In our stories, Lord Vishnu is the preserver, the one who steps in when the world's going off the rails. He doesn't show up the same way every time: he adapts, takes whatever form the crisis demands and restores balance.

Life works the same way. Every area—happiness, success, money, relationships, health—will face its own storm. If you want to move forward, you have to adapt. Not once. Not twice. Every single time.

That's why each Life Code in this book is inspired by one of Vishnu's avatars. Not as a sermon, but as a playbook for resilience, reinvention and balance.

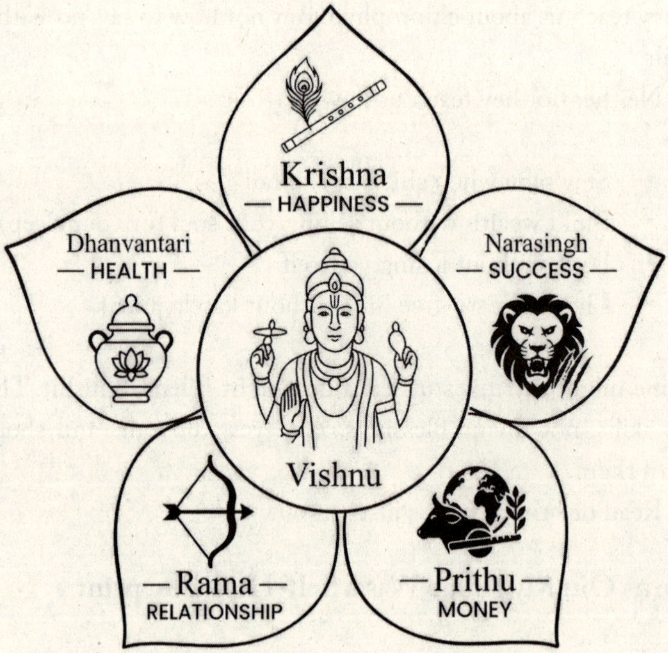

Happiness—Krishna: Experience joy and playfulness, even in chaos.
Success—Narsingh: Win the impossible game by changing how it's played.

Money—Prithu: Turn scarcity into abundance by creating systems that never stop giving.
Relationships—Rama: Practise loyalty, trust and dignity that lasts.
Health—Dhanvantari: Immerse yourself in healing, vitality and life in full power mode.

Vishnu's avatars manifested when balance went askew. This book is about calling on yours.

Knowledge isn't power. Applied knowledge is.

Reading won't change your life. Doing will. Even one sincere action beats a hundred pages skimmed.

SECTION 1
HAPPINESS

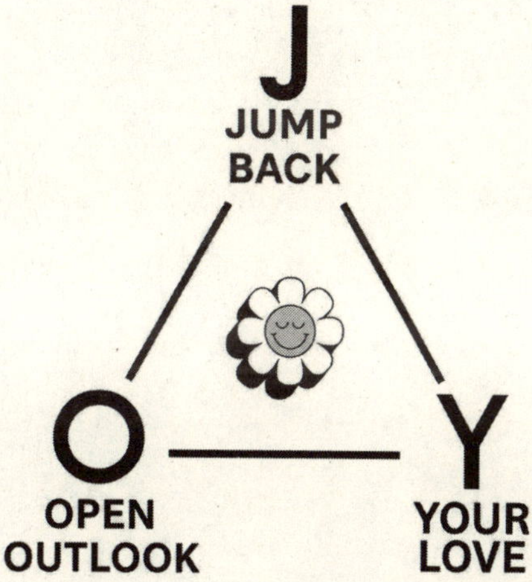

Inspired by Lord Krishna

Krishna played the flute in Vrindavan … and gave war strategy at Kurukshetra. With the same smile. He didn't wait for life to be perfect before being happy; he danced in the middle of chaos.

1

Stop 'MUSTerbating'!

'There is no way to happiness. Happiness is the way.'

—Buddha

(Also, that one uncle who dances at weddings like nobody's watching.)

6 March 2020. My company had just raised funding from Aishwarya Rai Bachchan. My start-up was valued at over ₹100 crore. I felt unstoppable.

Two weeks later, COVID-19 struck. The world shut down. Revenue became zero. And we had 400 employees to take care of. Investors took back their cheques. Then came the full Bollywood plot twist. My ex-wife filed multiple false cases against me—rape, dowry harassment, attempted murder. I was arrested and spent fifty days behind bars. (The Supreme Court quashed everything. This is a self-help book, not a crime thriller.)

But the story didn't end there. Of course not. I got fired from my own company, the one I'd built from scratch. It felt like hell. Some people said, 'Dude, you're like Steve Jobs.' Sure, except I had more hair.

And just when I thought I'd hit rock bottom, life whispered, '*Picture abhi baaki hai.*' I lost my father, my anchor. I didn't hug him long enough. We think there'll always be time—until there isn't.

Work. Marriage. My father. All gone. And with them, huge chunks of my identity.

There were nights I stared at the ceiling, unable to cry, unable to sleep. I felt my body lying in bed, but my soul seemed to have left the room. Even Netflix seemed to get me, constantly recommending *Eat, Pray, Love.* But in that stillness, something clicked: the world can take everything. But it can't take your power to begin again.

Choosing Happiness Anyway

I could have spiralled. Honestly, no one would've blamed me. There were mornings I didn't want to get out of bed. Hope felt like a scam. But I got up. Not because I was strong, but because I didn't want to stay broken forever.

Most days, I stayed hopeful, even happy. People were shocked. 'If you can still smile,' they'd say, 'what am I even complaining about?' I became an accidental inspiration simply by refusing to let darkness win.

How? Because pain is universal. But joy? Joy's a guest you have to invite in. I've learnt to cry, scream, sulk—whatever's needed. Then, I choose happiness. Not because I'm naïve, but because it's the one thing the world can't steal unless I hand it over. This book? It's your toolkit to choose it too.

The Trap of Conditional Happiness

The 2025 World Happiness Report ranks India 118th of 147 countries.[1] Most of us don't chase happiness, we chase permission to feel it. We tell ourselves: I must buy a house to be happy. I must lose weight. Get married. Go to Bali.

This is 'MUSTerbation', as psychologist Albert Ellis called it.[2] We stack 'musts' like a moral checklist, and until every box is ticked, we deny ourselves joy. But happiness isn't about what's missing. It's about noticing what's already here and choosing to see the good in it.

Your brain doesn't release dopamine only when you win an award. It also does so when you solve a puzzle, pet a dog, or when someone hugs you tight and doesn't let go.

American author Tony Robbins tells the story of two men in his book *Awaken the Giant Within*. Guy 1: 10 per cent body fat, but pissed because he wanted 8 per cent. Earns $1 million with a bonus, but is upset that it's not a fixed sum. He has three adorable kids, but he sulks because they don't behave exactly how he wants them to.

Guy 2: He's jumping with joy just because he can breathe. Despite all his struggles.

Both live on the same planet and breathe the same air. One's bitter. One's grateful. Who do you want to be? It's your call.[3]

Mic Drop: Joy Is Not a Trophy. It's a Torch

We don't suffer because life's hard. We suffer because of the scripts in our mind. Most weren't even written by us. Our schools, parents, Instagram, probably the fear of being nobody did that.

What if we stopped? Stopped waiting for abs. Stopped tying our worth to bank balances, emails or Bumble matches. Stopped

MUSTerbating. And started living. Joy doesn't wait at the finish line. It lights the damn path while you limp through it.

Should you be happy all the time? We'll talk about that in the next chapter. But for now? You just took the first step. That's rare. Be proud.

Do the Damn Thing: The Happiness Scale

Reflect: What MUST is stealing your joy right now?

Act: Burn it. Replace it with: *'I'm allowed joy. Not later. Now. Because I'm alive. And still showing up.'*

2

Sadness Isn't a Bug. It's a Feature

'The wound is the place where the Light enters you.'

— Rumi

If happiness is all we needed, the gods would've filled life with nothing but joy. But they didn't. From Buddha to Mahavira, from Krishna to Jesus, each one has taught us one blunt truth: sorrow is inevitable.

Each offered a way to hold it. Buddha said we should accept it. Mahavira said to renounce it. Jesus said, 'Endure it with hope.' And Krishna tells us to stay steady through it. None called sadness a weakness. They called it a teacher.

We hide pain behind 'I'm fine' texts and fake smiles. We treat sadness like spam—delete, ignore, move on. But sadness isn't noise. It's a system alert. Something's broken. Something inside you is asking to be heard.

A 2021 IIM Bangalore study says that 65 per cent of Indian youth overthink emotions, bottling sadness.[4] It's not weakness; it's your brain's signal to pause and process.

Why Some Sadness Is Actually Useful

Psychologist Dr Shefali Tsabary says, 'Sadness is your soul's GPS—listen to it.'[5] Feel it to heal it. Sadness isn't the villain. It's more like that brutally honest friend—irritating, but usually right.

You don't value light until you've sat in the dark. Not all lessons come from podcasts. Some arrive in silence.

For instance, take Sheryl Sandberg, former COO of Facebook. Top job. Two kids. Loving husband. Life looked perfect. Until one vacation, when her husband collapsed on a gym floor. He was gone in seconds.

Grief tore through her life. But instead of hiding, she wrote *Option B*, a book on rebuilding after loss. She didn't say, 'Think positive'. She said: 'We plant the seed of resilience in the way we process our sadness.'[6] That line has stayed with me.

You don't need to be hit by tragedy to take sadness seriously. Even small griefs need space.

First Principle, Boss! Why Sadness Slows Us Down

It's nature's way of making you rest, reflect and reset. Think of it as an emotional wound healing. Suppress it, and you limp forever. Sit with it and let it heal, and you walk stronger.

How I Used Unhappiness as a Guide

Between 2020 and 2023, my own life felt like a Netflix drama. There were nights I cried until I couldn't breathe. Days I couldn't eat or even get out of bed.

I cry even now. But I don't hide it anymore. (And yes, men are allowed to cry.) Because I've learnt that avoiding sadness doesn't make you strong. It makes you numb.

I kept moving—slow, angry, unsure. It was not easy and did not happen in a day. From that chaos, I rebuilt myself and my life one tiny, defiant step at a time:

- I signed up for nutrition courses. Not to save the world but to feel in control again.
- I built six-pack abs. Ran a half marathon. Not for Instagram but to remind myself I still had strength.
- I reconnected with my family on a whole new level—and finally realised just how much I'd taken them for granted.
- I started posting online. Not for fame but to turn pain into purpose.
- And slowly, I began writing this book. Because maybe—just maybe—someone out there needs these pages like I once did.

Even on my worst days, I stayed grateful. Not because life was all rainbows but because I focused on what was there. Small rituals helped. Gratitude journalling. Exercise. Surrendering when nothing made sense.

Sadness isn't a dead end. Sometimes, it's the damn doorway.

Stop Chasing Constant Happiness

If Chapter 1 showed you how to choose joy, this one is your permission slip for the days you just can't. The goal isn't to erase unhappiness. It's to stop being ashamed of it.

Cry. Scream. Sleep. Journal. Just don't stay stuck. Pain taught me how to pause. The next chapter? It's about how I learnt to move again.

Do the Damn Thing: The Joy Audit

Reflect: What emotion are you avoiding? Disappointment? Resentment? Hidden grief?

Label it. Naming it takes away half its power.

Act: Do one small thing that acknowledges it:

- Write about it in a journal
- Share it with a friend
- Go for a walk without your phone, and just *feel* for once

Bonus: Ask: '*What is this feeling trying to teach me?*' Most emotions are messengers. If you listen, they stop shouting.

3

Failure = Foreplay! You Are Just Getting Started

'Obstacles don't block the path. They are the path.'

—*Zen proverb*

The list was pinned to the wall. A4 sheet. Black ink. Eleven names. His wasn't on it—again. His friends were heartbroken. He wasn't. That night, he threw a party. No speeches. Just chai, samosas. 'Today's rejection means I need to work harder. This party will remind me not to forget that.'

He didn't treat failure like a slap in the face. He treated it like a signal to rise. That boy lifted the 2007 and 2011 Cricket World Cups. But the real win? He celebrated even on the days he lost. Today, we call him Thala. But back then, he was just another boy from Ranchi who refused to sulk.

What if you also raised a toast to your 'L', your losses? What if you didn't hide your failures but wore them like armour?

It's natural to feel crushed after failure. Pain wears many faces—loss, rejection, disappointment. And the first question that hits us is always: *'Why me? Why this much?'*

But here's the reframe: Pain is a privilege. Pressure isn't punishment—it's preparation. The same force that crushes coal also creates diamonds. Life doesn't throw weight at you to break you. It does so to expand your capacity to endure it. And it never gives you more than you can carry.

Every time I've experienced a lot of pressure—days where I thought I'd collapse—I have come out sharper, clearer and more powerful. Failure has been the entry ticket to growth. Always.

A life coach once asked in one of his workshops: 'What happens to your energy when life punches you?' Most people said: 'It drops like a stone.' I said: 'It rises like a fire.' Because when life knocks me down, a voice inside whispers: 'This is where your story begins.'

We all want to be heroes. But most of us want to skip the villain arc. Unfortunately, it doesn't work that way.

My Boss Tried to Kill My Dreams. I Thanked Him

Right after graduation, I landed my dream consulting job. But I was quietly nursing a bigger dream—IIM. So I started prepping. Some days I skipped dinner. Some nights, I skipped sleep. There were moments I thought, 'Maybe this is enough. Maybe I should stop.' But something deeper—maybe desperation, maybe defiance—kept me going.

Then came the results of the Common Admission Test: I had got interview calls from all the IIMs. I was ecstatic. The happiest day of my life. I told my boss about it, but he didn't celebrate. 'I do not want you to leave the company and I will make sure you flunk your interviews. I'll bury you in work. And all your leaves are cancelled. Let's see how you crack the interviews.'

Everybody advised me to quit. I would have to anyway quit in four months after passing the interview stage. Why jeopardise my chances of securing IIM admissions?

But I didn't. If I had quit, it would have meant I was backing down from my boss's challenge. And I don't back down. He said I wouldn't be able to handle work and interview prep. I decided to make the challenge even more difficult: why just those two things? I would do three things. And the third would be far more difficult than the first two: write a book (and that too on economics).

My writing skills? Trash. My knowledge of the book's topic: zilch. It made no sense. But twenty-two-year-old irrational exuberance doesn't need sense.

The result: I cracked IIM-A, my manager admitted I was too good for him and somehow Macmillan published my book, making me one of the youngest economics authors in the world. I sent my boss a copy with a note: 'This book happened because of you. Thank you.' I was not being sarcastic. Just true. He didn't destroy me. He introduced me to a version of myself I hadn't met before.

Flip the Script: Failure Is Fake News

We treat failure like it's final. But what if it's just … feedback? Edison '*failed*' 1,000 times. Oprah got fired. Elon was mocked. They didn't give up. They co-created with failure.

Imagine life like a water filter. Success pours in, but failure is the charcoal—it removes the BS. It's what sharpens your instincts. Cuts the fluff. Trains focus. Reminds you what actually matters. Your failures aren't a waste. They're refiners.

As Krishna says in the Gita—no effort on the right path is ever wasted.[7] Even the smallest step matters, and protects you from fear. That's why failure isn't final. The effort itself transforms you, even if the result takes time.

Failure isn't here to end your story. It's here to make your comeback iconic. You're not breaking. You're becoming. And sometimes, becoming means asking for help. Not because you're weak—but because you're done playing solo. Let's talk about that next.

4

Therapy Is the New Six-Pack

'I wasn't mad. I was just sad, anxious, sleep-deprived, overworked and spiralling at 2 a.m. But sure —"mad" sounds easier.'

My friend once stared at a therapist's number for weeks. Thumb on dial. Ego on full volume. 'Do I really need therapy?' 'Am I crazy?' 'Isn't therapy just for people who've fully lost it?'

Welcome to India, where going to therapy is still seen as a personal failure. A 2022 study by the National Institute of Mental Health and Neurosciences (NIMHANS) says 150 million Indians need mental health support, but only 30 per cent seek it due to stigma.[8] And most still think mental health tips = do yoga, take a trip, marry a nice girl/boy.

A friend said, 'Bro, just take a vacation.' I felt like replying, 'Bro, I'm anxious in Goa too.'

When you carry your chaos inside, even the most peaceful place feels like a prison.

When Arjun froze on the battlefield, he didn't Google '5 hacks for confidence'. He asked for help—and Krishna became his therapist.

If your tooth hurts, you go to a dentist. Not a DJ. If you're diabetic, you don't chant affirmations. You get a damn doctor. Why not do the same for mental health?

Here is a fun fact (actually, not so fun): Cognitive Behavioural Therapy (CBT) works. Science says it rewires your brain.[9] Like going to the gym.

Mumbai-based therapist Dr Hvovi Bhagwagar says, 'Therapy's like a haircut for your mind—regular upkeep keeps you sharp.' Start with small steps to vibe higher.

Dear Zindagi, Thank You

Alia Bhatt's character in *Dear Zindagi* is successful. Talented. Falling apart. Shah Rukh Khan plays her therapist. And his guidance comes in the form of metaphors. Space. And a mirror.

> *'You try out chairs before buying one. So why not relationships?'*
> *'You can't choose how your story begins. But you can choose how to end it.'*

That's therapy. Not magic. Just method. Not erasing pain. Just learning how to hold it without bleeding all over everyone. Therapy is not a weakness. It's not for broken people. It's for brave people. Athletes have coaches. Founders have mentors. Why should you figure it all out alone? The strongest sentence you'll ever say: 'I need help.'

'But Therapy Is Expensive, Bro'

Yes. It is. So is ignoring your mental health and burning out at thirty-two. If you can pay your monthly instalments for your iPhone, you can plan for three sessions with a therapist. Your brain deserves more than just Wi-Fi and caffeine.

Anita from Guwahati, a civil services aspirant, felt crushed by exam stress. She tried Wysa's free AI chats, then found a counsellor via her college, turning anxiety into action.

You ask for help with passwords. With Excel sheets. With parking spots. But not with the one thing that actually matters—your peace. It's not weak to ask. It's wise. Healing is a flex. Use it. Asking for help is step one. But step two? Noticing what's still good.

Do the Damn Thing: Brain ka Band-Aid

Reflect: What's one issue that has been bothering you for a long time?

Act: Imagine you've won three free therapy sessions. Would you go? If yes, find a way to take that first step this month. Or talk to ChatGPT/Wysa as a therapist. Seriously. It may not have a couch, but it's cheaper, always available and won't judge your daddy issues. Just don't confuse it for a real person.

5

7,000 People Died This Hour. You Didn't. Now What?

It's not happiness that brings us gratitude. It's gratitude that brings us happiness.

Let's say you wake up one day and land up in jail. Without committing any crime. That was me. I had every reason to be pissed. To scream. To spiral. To lose faith in everything. And for a while, I did.

But in that darkness, something cracked open. I started a gratitude journal from my jail cell. Not because I was wise, but because I needed something to hold on to. I was thankful for:

- A family that stood by me like a rock
- A healthy body that still carried me
- Access to a library and books, even inside jail
- Everything life had always given me.

One major blow didn't erase the hundreds of things still working.

Because even in hell, I realised that not everything was burning. And that tiny shift? It saved me.

We think gratitude is for 'good times'. But real gratitude isn't tested when life's sweet. It's tested when life punches you.

You don't need to be in jail to feel trapped. Some are imprisoned by heartbreak. Some by their boss's 11 p.m. Slack messages. Gratitude feels impossible in those moments. But that's when it counts the most.

Be grateful for all the pressures and pains. As I said earlier, pressure is a privilege. Pain gives you purpose. It's the universe's way of making you stronger. To create a better life for you.

Humans are wired for negativity. It's called negativity bias. One insult sticks longer than ten compliments. One pimple ruins your mood, even if your whole face is glowing.[10]

We obsess over the one bad review and ignore the hundred five-stars. We scroll Instagram not to smile—but to compare. Not 'What do I have?' but 'Why don't I have that?'

Gratitude flips that script. It doesn't deny pain. It holds space for both: the ache and the awe. Gratitude in pain is protest. It's the middle finger you show life—with a smile.

Proof: Nick Vujicic

At age ten, he tried to drown himself. The water was calm. The pain was not. He held his breath. But his will to die wasn't stronger than his parents' love.

He surfaced. Gasping. Crying.

Years later, he stood on a stage. No arms. No legs. Finally having accepted tetra-amelia syndrome, a condition where he was born without any of his limbs. People asked, 'How do you stay positive?'

He lifted his only limb—a tiny foot with two toes—and placed it gently on the mic. 'I just started being thankful for this,' he said.

Someone in the front row laughed. Then cried. He never asked to be a miracle. But once he stopped asking 'why me', he became one. Gratitude doesn't solve problems. It makes you strong enough to face them.[11]

Imagine you're a deer. The jungle is your Zomato. But every sip of water is a ticket in the death lottery. A predator is already eyeing you for lunch.

And your baby? Most likely won't even make it past six months.

That's stress. That's hardship. That's life with antlers instead of Wi-Fi.

Now look at us. We rage if the air conditioning stops for ten minutes. Maybe it's time we stop complaining and start noticing the obvious—life is ridiculously safe, ridiculously precious. And we take it for granted every day.

A ten-week study by psychologists Robert A. Emmons and Michael E. McCullough showed that people who journalled gratitude felt 25 per cent more optimistic. Their health improved too.[12]

Science calls it neuroplasticity. Ancient India called it Santosha—the quiet art of enough.[13]

So say thank you. Out loud. Don't be a miser.

Liked the food? Thank the cook. Or the Swiggy delivery person.

Someone helped you today? Text them.

Love someone's smile? Compliment them.

Liked a reel? Drop a kind comment—not just heart-eye emojis. Appreciation is free dopamine. And it boomerangs. You don't need a perfect life to feel grateful. You just need perspective. Start there.

The next chapter? It's about forgiveness. And no, it doesn't mean gifting your ex a teddy bear. (Or does it?)

Do the Damn Thing: Gratitude Gym

Reflect: What's *one* tiny thing you're grateful for today?

Act: Send one message. Voice note. Compliment. Make someone's day—and yours.

Bonus Rep: Start a gratitude journal. And write three good things that happened to you in the last twenty-four hours. Remember—7,000 people just died in the last hour. You didn't.

Don't flip the page unless you actually feel grateful.

Reading this book won't help.
Doing something about it will.

6

Thank Your Enemies (Yes, Seriously)

'Holding a grudge is like hugging a cactus and blaming the plant.'

Imagine if actor Prabhas actually ghosted his colleague Sathyaraj in real life. Just because Katappa killed Baahubali in their movie.

Sounds crazy, right? But we do the same. We carry grudges. As if the other person is the villain, not just playing one.

Someone cheated? Lied? Hurt you? They were just cast as the villain for that scene. Too good at their role? Sure. Still, it's just a role.

Some people drag on emotional problems for decades like it's designer baggage.

Don't Just Forgive, Thank the Damn Villain

Would *Baahubali* be even half the hit it was without Katappa's betrayal? Would there be a Lord Ram without a Raavan? Or a Batman without a Joker?

Hell, even milk needs lemon or vinegar to go from 'bland milk' to 'party starter'. No villain = No hero.

So if you want to be the main character (and you do), pray for stronger enemies. And if you can't do that, at least don't crib about one.

Most people hate their enemies. Some 'evolved' ones forgive. You? You're going to thank them. Yep! Thank them for the chaos, the heartbreak, the identity crisis.

They were your karmic gym trainers. They made you level up.

Let me give you one real-life example: Malala Yousafzai. Just a schoolgirl in Pakistan who wanted to study.

Her enemy? The Taliban. One of their gunmen shot her in the head. At point blank range. For wanting to study.

The plot twist? She didn't die. She rose. Oxford. Nobel Peace Prize. Millions of girls empowered.

She didn't just forgive him—she thanked him. Not with words. But with her transformation.

'I used to think the Talib would come, and I would have a gun ... but then I thought: if you hit a Talib with your shoe, what's the difference between you and him?'[14]

That's not weakness. That's God-level strength. Turning bullets into books. Trauma into torchlight. She didn't just survive her villain—she outgrew him. That's something heroes do.

When my ex filed cases against me, it didn't turn me bitter. It made me better. I never trash-talked her—even when people expected me to.

She wasn't my enemy. She was just a co-actor ... in a scene neither of us fully wrote. And God—bless Him—didn't cast me in the negative role.

Today, I genuinely thank her. Why? For my Salman Khan phase—remote in one hand, peace in the other. I don't fight over what's for dinner. My clothes live on the bed rent-free. And the bathroom seat? It stays up unapologetically.

On a serious note, that chaos made me 10x stronger. This book exists because of that fire. What looked like the worst thing turned out to be the best thing.

Sri Sri Ravi Shankar says, 'Forgiveness is not for the other person. It's for you—to set yourself free from the burden of anger.'[15] Forgiveness doesn't mean you turn into a doormat. If someone's actions demand consequences, they should face them. Justice and forgiveness can co-exist.

You forgive to walk free. To stop playing the scene on loop in your mind. Let the law do its job. But don't let the villain stay in your mind rent-free.

A Harvard study found that holding grudges = low immunity, high anxiety, weak heart.[16] Basically, emotional poison with zero benefits. It's like dragging around a 20-kilo invisible backpack … and wondering why life feels heavy.

Want mythological proof? Meet Karna. Skilled. Loyal. Dripping with potential. But he carried every insult like it came with cashback. His grudges didn't just kill his joy—they killed him in the end. Proof that enemies don't destroy you. Your grudges do.

Send a Thank You Card

Not a revenge plot. Not a middle finger. Send a thank-you card. Or a teddy bear. Not because they earned it—but because you've healed. (Only if you're ready. Most aren't. And that's okay.)

Let them see it every day and go: 'Damn. I messed with the wrong peaceful psycho.'

Because life's too short to hold grudges. And honestly? Most people don't even know why they do what they do. Shock them with your grace. They'll call you crazy. Good. Join the tribe. Normal is overrated.

And when the play ends? Everyone takes a bow. Even the villain. Don't carry the pain. Carry the plot twist.

Do the Damn Thing: Channel Your Inner Geet (*Jab We Met* Style)

Reflect: Who still lives rent-free in your head?

Act: Write them a letter. Say everything you never said. No filters. No 'be the bigger person' crap. Then burn it (safely). Watch the ashes and say, 'You don't control my peace anymore.'

7

Surrender, Drama Queen

'Yesterday is history. Tomorrow is a mystery. Today? A damn gift.'
—Master Oogway, Philosopher in a Turtle Suit
(in his Gen Z Avatar)

Usain Bolt, the fastest man on Earth, runs at 45 km/hr. But guess what? You—yes, the chai-sipping, 'what-if' machine that you are—are already moving at 8,00,000 km/hr.

I'm not kidding. And no, I haven't smoked anything weird. Earth spins at a speed of 1,600 km/hr. It zooms around the Sun at 1,07,000 km/hr. And the Sun itself races through the galaxy at 7,20,000 km/hr.[17]

So even when you're in bed, spiralling over an awkward message from 2018, you're already zooming through the universe. And yet we live like we're supposed to control everything—from our careers to our crush's mood swings.

Why Are You Acting Like the CEO of the Universe?

We didn't pick our parents. Our country. Our height. Our genes. Yet we stress about everything—as if Lord Krishna outsourced karma management to us.

Even He said in the Gita: 'Do your karma, but the results aren't yours to own.'[18] Boom. It's the biggest lesson of the Gita.

It teaches us to surrender. But is surrender like giving up? No, it's giving over. Surrender doesn't mean doing nothing. It means doing your part—and letting go of what was never yours.

You can row the boat. But you can't control the tide. You can water the plant. But you can't force it to flower overnight.

Michael Singer's *The Surrender Experiment* made me rethink hustle culture.[19] Sometimes, peace is found not in doing more—but in letting go.

We overthink because we think it's all on us. Surrender is remembering that it's not. Surrender doesn't mean giving up control. It means accepting we never had it to begin with.

Assuming I have immense control over my life, I've directed dozens of mental movies in my head. Spoiler: 99 per cent of these films never got released. But damn, the production budget? Sky-high. Overthinking feels productive. But it's just your brain running fake rehearsals for imaginary disasters.

Imagine this: a wooden plank, 8 inches wide placed on the ground. You walk across it easily. Now, take that same plank and put it between two skyscrapers. What happens? You freeze. Panic. Pee a little.

Same plank. Same legs. What changed? Your thoughts.

We live life like we're walking on air. But in reality, we're safe only on solid ground. What's that one thought you've been spiralling over? Now imagine it's just a wooden plank on the ground. Tell it: 'Chill, bro.' And walk past.

First Principle, Boss! Why We Overthink

Overthinking isn't a character flaw. It's your brain's way of rehearsing danger—a leftover survival tool from when danger meant death. But in today's world, it creates stress, not safety. Train your brain to pause, not panic.

WTF Moments in My Life

I thought I was running the whole damn show. Until life humbled me with creepy astrology 'spoilers'.

My jail episode? Predicted months in advance—by an astrologer who knew nothing about me or my ex. He even said, 'Your current wife will give you the toughest time.' Boom. Timeline matched.

And this prediction wasn't a one-off. My IIM-A admission. A stalker who troubled me for eighteen months. Different astrologers. Different cities. Same eerie accuracy.

Call it astrology. Call it destiny. Call it freak coincidence. But when enough of those predictions hit, I stopped pretending I had complete control over my life. That's when surrender stopped sounding like weakness. And became the only thing that made sense.

Surrender > Control

Even your 'free will' isn't fully free. Most of what you call 'you' is just pre-installed programming reacting to inputs. Humans are algorithms made of flesh.

Your brain fires thoughts before you're even aware of them. So no, you're not the CEO. You're more like middle management—with good intentions but limited control. Which makes surrender not just spiritual advice … but the only logical move left on the board.

So, be *Here Now*. Not *Three Years Later*. The brain is a time-travelling monkey—always swinging between 'What if?' and 'Oh no.'

Peace isn't in your five-year plan. It's in your five-minute breath. Control screams: 'Fix everything.' Surrender whispers: 'Do your part. Then let go.' One leads to panic. The other to peace.

You're already spinning at 8,00,000 km/hr. Maybe your thoughts don't need to spin too.

In the next chapter, we turn the camera to something fun: what if life wasn't a burden … but a biopic? Grab your popcorn.

~~Do the Damn Thing~~ Be the Damn Space

Reflect: What thought loop keeps hijacking your peace?

Act: Meditate. Close your eyes. Inhale for 4 seconds, hold for 4, exhale for 6. Do this for 5 rounds. With every breath out, imagine dropping a suitcase of junk you've carried for years.

8

Play the Hero. It's Your Badass Biopic

'At the end of every movie, there is always a happy ending. And if the ending is not happy, then the movie is not over yet.'

—Shah Rukh Khan

Would you pay ₹300 to watch a movie where the hero never struggles, the villain takes a sabbatical and nothing goes wrong?

Exactly. That's not a film. That's a screensaver.

But now flip the camera to your own life—and suddenly, you want smooth, perfect, no-plotline peace. Sorry, that's not how blockbusters are made.

Your life? It's a full-blown masala biopic. And guess who's the lead? (Clue: You're not 'Bystander #6' holding the hero's coffee.)

Heartbreak? That's your tragic romance arc. Public failure? Classic pre-climax dip. That night you ugly-cried alone? National Award scene.

Even Karan Johar would say, 'Damn, this script has depth.' So the next time life slaps you sideways, don't ask, 'Why me?' Ask, 'Interval ho gaya kya?'

Plot Twist = Plot Worth Watching

Here's the brutal truth: If your life has no drama, nobody's watching it. Not even you. The best stories have pain, betrayal, breakdowns—and then comebacks.

Mine? You've heard it all. Just add an item number and background score, and we have box office gold.

Let me give you a real story that would be a blockbuster: Arunima Sinha. National-level volleyball player. Pushed out of a moving train. One leg lost. Dreams shattered. Most people would've hit pause. Not her. From a hospital bed, she set a new goal—climb Mount freaking Everest.

Not walk again. Not recover. But climb Everest. With a prosthetic leg. Everyone thought she was delusional. She trained anyway. Fell. Bled. Got back up.

Two years later, she stood on top of the world. The first female amputee to summit Everest. No music. No director. Just raw grit. That's what a hero arc looks like. Plot twist → Plot upgrade.[20]

Switching to Game Mode

Life isn't just a movie. It's also a video game. The goal isn't peace. It's the chase. The chase gives us a purpose to play the game of our life every day. If there's no chase, no struggle, no purpose, life becomes stagnant.

A friend once got too philosophical and said, 'I have enough money. I just want to chill and do nothing.' He enjoyed the silence at first. Morning walks. Long naps. Insta scrolls. But within months rest turned into restlessness. No chase. No struggle. No fun.

Thankfully, he set new goals. Started volunteering. Mentoring others. And just like that, he found his fire again.

We enjoy a game despite the losses. And restart again. Why should life be any different? Play for fun, not just results. Every new challenge is just the next level. And the player with the most resets usually wins.

Cry Dramatically, then Cut to Your Comeback

Your life becomes the story you believe about yourself. Psychologists call it 'narrative identity'. Think like a hero—not a victim. Even if you're bleeding, even if the Wi-Fi's down, even if your crush left you. Be the damn main character.

There's this bald, brainy Israeli historian called Yuval Noah Harari. Wrote *Sapiens*. Went viral for saying humans ruled the world not through muscles but stories. Not love stories. Belief stories. According to him, religions, companies, countries are just collective fiction we all agree to believe in.[21]

So if you're stuck in a sad little story where you say, 'I'm not enough' or 'It's too late for me' ... that's just Season 1. Flip the script. Because narratives aren't facts. They're editable Netflix plots.

Ancient Indian bonus: even gods treated life as a leela—a divine play. Nothing is as serious or permanent as it feels. So if they can treat life as a game, maybe you can loosen up about your boss's passive-aggressive email.

Some days, life is a movie. Some days, a game. Either way, you're not here just to survive. You're here to star. So, lights. Camera. Action. Don't just deliver your lines. Deliver your moment. Every great movie has a breakdown. But only legends turn it into a breakthrough.

Still crying over the plot twist? Don't worry—Karan Johar is already auditioning your script. In the next chapter, we flip the script to words.

9

Your Mouth, the Chief Mood Officer

'If you don't like something, change it. If you can't change it, change your attitude.'

—*Maya Angelou*

'Ugh, traffic.'
'My boss is Hitler's cousin.'
'Why is the weather having mood swings again?'

If cribbing was a sport, Indians would dominate with gold medals. Then we'd complain the medal doesn't match our kurta.

But complaining doesn't change the world. It just changes your mood—for the worse. Why do we complain then? Because it gives us fake control. Because it's a cheap substitute for action.

Anupam Kher once told a story that's been looping in my brain like a stuck Spotify ad. He was on a film set in

Chennai. It was hot enough to fry an egg on the pavement. He was sweating, annoyed with the heat and the defunct air-conditioner.

Then he saw superstar Amitabh Bachchan sitting calmly in a full suit, wig, makeup and a blanket. With no fan, no AC. Just chilling and reading a book.

Anupam was puzzled. He asked, 'Sir, don't you feel hot?' Big B smiled and said slowly: 'If I think about the heat, I'll feel hot. If I don't, I won't.'

That one line? Retired my inner whiner for good. Turns out, most discomfort is a decision—powered by your words.

Cribbing Is Killing Your Brain

Stanford research says that chronic complaining can shrink your hippocampus.[22] That's the part that helps you solve problems and remember stuff. Basically, the more you whine, the worse you get at fixing anything. Now that's some cosmic irony.

It's like yelling at the Wi-Fi router when the electricity's gone. It's useless and draining. So I made a deal with myself: I won't crib about what I can't control. Not traffic. Not the weather. Not my hair on humid days. Instead of fuming in traffic, I listen to podcasts. Instead of ranting about politics, I try to vote, donate or shut up.

I found this gem called the 'No Cribs Challenge' in *The 4-Hour Workweek* by Tim Ferriss.[23] Simple. Brutal. Effective. Wear a rubber band on your wrist. Goal: twenty-one days of no complaining. If you slip up, switch wrists and restart from Day 1. Even if you were on Day 20. Even if your chai spilled and your ex texted, 'Hey :)'. Start over.

It took me months to finish. But it rewired my brain.

Reframe Your Words to Redesign Your World

Your words shape your world. They are energy. And mood-shapers. They're not harmless. They're hammers. Or hugs.

Say 'I hate this day' enough times, and your brain starts to believe it. Reframe your phrases. Instead of 'people are so dumb', try 'people are ... vibing differently'.

You don't have to lie to yourself. But you can choose softer truths. You're not being fake. You're just choosing sanity over sass. Here's my favourite cheat sheet:

Negative	Reframed
Stubborn	Persistent
Hyper	Energetic
Stingy	Mindful spender
Gullible	Trusting
Careless	Carefree

Small swaps = massive energy shift. The Mahabharata agrees: 'He who conquers his tongue conquers his mind.' Big flex, honestly.

Mic Drop: Rise Above Petty Problems

We all want to be 'Level 10' humans. But we burn out solving Level 2 problems. Traffic. Gossip. Weather.

Small loops. Small lives. If your mind keeps returning to the same petty drama, maybe it doesn't want peace. Maybe it wants familiarity. So, the next time your brain wants to rant—pause. Take a breath. Say something lighter. Your peace depends on it.

Now let's talk about the most underrated mood medicine: laughter. Even if it starts with a bad pun.

Do the Damn Thing: Rewire the Rant

Reflect: What's your go-to complaint—and what's beneath it?

Act: Wear a string or band on your wrist. Each time you complain, switch hands. Try going twenty-four hours without moving it.

10

Laugh, Dammit

'A person without a sense of humour is like a wagon without springs. It's jolted by every pebble on the road.'

—Henry Ward Beecher

If laughter had a LinkedIn profile, it would read: 'Breaks tension. Builds connection. Wins job offers.' Let me prove it.

How I Got a Job by Laughing to Their Face

I was sweating through an interview with a top London bank at IIM-A. Tense panel. High stakes. Suited sharks.

The interviewer asked, 'If every company selects you, which one will you join?' I smiled and said, 'Your company.'

And then I laughed. Not a chuckle. A full, awkward, 'oops-I-laughed-too-much' laugh.

He raised an eyebrow: 'Why are you laughing?' I said, 'Because I've told the same lie to seven companies today.'

Silence. Awkward pause. Me mentally Googling 'How to sell samosas with an MBA'.

Then came the plot twist: he cursed, called every other interviewer in, and said, 'Usually we have five interview rounds. But I like your honesty and humour. I'm giving you the offer right now. And if you don't take it, we won't come to IIM-A next year.'

That's how I got the first offer on campus that year. Not because of my scores. But because I dared to joke when others were dying to impress.

Why Humour Works Everywhere

Humour isn't a luxury. It's a survival skill. Life is full of speed breakers, and humour is your suspension. Without it, life's bumps will rattle your soul like a cheap Uber ride.

- **Breaks the ice:** I once told a girl on a date, 'I run a start-up.' She said, 'That's okay. Not everyone is picked up in the placement rounds.' We both laughed. The ice melted. So did my ego.
- **Handles trauma:** After jail, a friend asked how I could still smile. I said, 'My in-laws gave me jail tourism in dowry. It was an all-inclusive package.' Sometimes humour isn't a mask, it's oxygen.
- **Softens criticism:** Someone once told me, 'Your IG video has no depth.' I replied, 'Just like my dating life.' We laughed. I cried later. Balance was restored.
- **Delays botox:** People say I look twenty-nine at forty-three. I say, 'That's still old. My mental age is twelve.'

- **Heals faster than gyaan:** Friend: 'I feel like a failure.' Me: 'Same, bro. At least we're consistent.' He smiled. Pain didn't vanish, but it loosened its grip.

And if you can't laugh at your own mess, call me. I probably can.

First Principle, Boss! Why Laugher Is Survival Software

In tribal times, laughter signalled safety and connection. That's why dark jokes during tough times *work*. Laughter lowers cortisol, boosts immunity and bonds people faster than a TED Talk. So no, it's not a waste of time. It's emotional CPR.[24]

Lord Krishna didn't give TED Talks. He stole butter. Danced on pots. Flirted with gopis. Basically, he was the OG prankster. Even God didn't take life too seriously. Why are you?

Laugh more. Sulk less. I'd rather be called childish and stay happy than be mature, composed ... and dead inside.

You don't need to be a stand-up comic. Just someone who doesn't take things personally. In meetings. In mistakes. In marriages.

The world is already heavy AF. You? Be the damn helium balloon.

Laughing for 15 minutes burns 40 calories. So technically, Hotstar + stand-up = cardio. Eat that, treadmill.

And if you haven't laughed till your stomach hurt in weeks, maybe that's what you're missing. Not a new job. Not a partner. Not another reel about 'how billionaires wake up at 4 a.m.'

Maybe all you need is one guilt-free, ugly-face, snort-filled laugh. But can a poor person afford to take life lightly? Let's find out.

Do the Damn Thing: Be the Lighter One

Reflect: When was the last time you laughed till your stomach ached?

Act: Watch your favourite comedy tonight. Laugh like nobody's judging. And if someone does, laugh harder.

11

Do You Know About Your ₹45-crore Asset?

Crorepati. Clueless. Classic combo.

Welcome to today's WTF Auction. First item on sale: a pair of working eyes. Perfect 6/6 vision. Starting bid: ₹50 lakh.

Next: a heart that beats 1,00,000 times a day. Never calls in sick. Bid starts at ₹1 crore.

And finally, a fully loaded brain. Includes creativity, logic, anxiety and overthinking. No returns.

Suddenly, it hits you—they're auctioning your body. You scream: 'STOP! This isn't for sale!'

Exactly. If you wouldn't sell your eyes for ₹50 lakh, or your heart for a crore, you're already a multi-crorepati. Congratulations!

Stop Sleeping on Your Fortune

You've been sitting on crores. Not in stocks. Not in crypto. But in breath, bones and badass biology.

Rough estimates say if you priced your body part-by-part, you'd be worth tens of crores. That's without counting the real gold: your childhood memories. That one friend who laughs like a donkey. Your ability to fall in love at a red light.

You're not broke. You're just undervaluing the assets that don't show up on a balance sheet. But here's the real kicker: we sit on assets worth crores … and cry about thousands. Like someone who owns a Ferrari, but complains about petrol prices. Or a guy with gold bars under his bed begging for a ₹10 PayTM cashback.

If Mukesh Ambani gave you a ₹50-crore machine and said, 'Bhai, this is your one shot. Use it well,' would you not take extra care of it?

Exactly. Your body is that machine. You're just too distracted to read the instruction manual.

Health = Happiness (Yes, It's That Simple)

Here's the wild part: science says health isn't just about living longer—it's about living happier. A 2023 global study found that people who exercise regularly are 43 per cent happier than those who don't.[25] Harvard's eighty-year happiness study also says that poor health in midlife predicts not just an early death but a miserable one.[26]

The World Happiness Report shows health is one of the top three drivers of life satisfaction—right up there with money and relationships.[27] Skip health, and you're basically short-circuiting your happiness engine.

So, your ₹45-crore body? It's not just money in the bank. It's mood in the bank.

I once met a man who lost his voice after a stroke. He didn't miss giving speeches. He missed singing 'Chanda Hai Tu' to his daughter at bedtime. That's real wealth. The kind we forget … until it disappears.

So the next time you feel broke or behind in life, pause. Put your hand on your heart. Feel it beat? That's a ₹1-crore reminder—you've already won the damn lottery. Start living like it.

Up next: But what's the realest wealth of all? Let's talk about people. And love.

12

Ghost the Killer Bros. Unlock Your Joy

'Comparison is the thief of joy. Expectation is its cousin.'
—Theodore Roosevelt

Ask a chaiwala how Virat Kohli should bat, how Narendra Modi should govern or how Mukesh Ambani should invest—and he'll give you an extensive TED Talk. But ask him how to improve his tea? Suddenly … he's too busy to listen to you.

That's the problem. We have too many expectations from the world, and too few from ourselves.

Now add his younger brother: comparison. She's wearing Zara, but my bank balance says. '*Zaraa soch le.*'

Comparison starts quietly. It's initially harmless. But one scroll later, you hate your job, your jeans and your jawline.

These two brothers don't knock. They just walk in, open your fridge, eat your peace and vanish. It's time to throw them out.

Expect Less from Others. Expect More from Yourself

'The movie was okay. But not as good as *Baahubali*.' Sure, bro. Not every movie has to have a fight with 10,000 people in slow motion.

High expectations = high chance of disappointment. I keep my bar low. It helps me enjoy life more.

For me, there are two kinds of movies: good or very good. I like all movies. Even *Tashan*. I've watched it twice. With sunglasses. In a cinema hall. That was my Tashan.

I'm not saying we should accept nonsense. But maybe like more things than we hate. Zero expectations is a myth. Even monks expect the bell to ring on time. The goal isn't to erase expectations. It's to hold them lightly. Like balloons—not bricks.

Keep the bar flexible for others, but set it high for yourself. Success? It's still your job. Standards? Yes, they still matter.

We expect life to follow our script. You order butter paneer. Life serves jeera aloo. Now you've got two choices. Crib and ruin your meal. Or taste it and realise that jeera aloo isn't bad at all.

That's life. It doesn't care about your order slip. It sends what it wants, when it wants. The problem isn't life's surprises. It's our refusal to enjoy them.

Maybe the real glow-up is learning to accept—not expect.

Jim Carrey once said, 'I wish everyone could get rich and famous … so they'd realise it's not the answer.' He had it all. Money. Fame. Awards. Laughter. And yet, he battled depression for years.

That's the thing about expectations—they never learn to say, 'Enough.' And if expectations weren't enough, their younger, sneakier cousin—comparison—just makes it worse. Comparison doesn't shout, it just stings quietly.

Comparison Is a Scam. Stop Buying In

Comparison isn't about other people. It's about you feeling less—and blaming their highlight reel. You see their salary, not their stress. Their wedding pictures, not their fights. Their glow-up, not their gut issues.

Comparison is not envy. It's an identity crisis. You don't want their life. You just forgot what yours is about. When you scroll through others' feeds, you're not jealous. You're just lost.

> **First Principle, Boss! Why We Compare**
>
> Comparison exists because humans evolved in tribes. Your brain is wired to constantly track your position in the social hierarchy—for survival.

A friend of mine has a multi-crore net worth. Flies business class like it's an auto rickshaw. But he can't sleep, sit or walk without pain.

His Instagram feed shows a millionaire life. His reality looks like a rehab centre. So should I feel jealous of his money … or grateful for my working knees?

I choose my knees. Every. Single. Time.

People often feel jealous of those born into rich or famous families—like Arjun Tendulkar or Abhishek Bachchan. But think again. Do they really deserve your envy … or your sympathy?

Even if they don't want to compare themselves with their dads, the world doesn't stop. It keeps reminding them they're smaller. If they were born in an ordinary family and achieved the same things, we'd call them super achievers. But under the shadow of a giant, their success looks tiny.

In ancient times or modern, comparison has always stolen peace.

In the Mahabharata, Yaksha asked Yudhishthira, 'Who is the happiest person?' He didn't say the richest. Or the smartest. He said: 'The one who is content.'[28]

And me? I still expect. I still compare. But now, I treat expectations and comparison like unwanted guests. I greet them, smile and show them the door. When you stop watching reels of other people's lives, you start showing up in your own. Fully. Freely. Finally.

13

Hugs > Hustle

'Treasure your relationships, not your possessions.'

—Anthony J. D'Angelo

Harvard University studied happiness for eighty-five years. And who turned out to be the big winner? Not money. Not status. Not six-packs or six-figure jobs. Just this: relationships.[29]

Still, what's the first thing we ditch when chasing success? Our people. We skip birthdays but attend back-to-back Zoom calls. We say 'bro for life' but ghost them by Diwali. Research confirms this: a 2023 Pew India survey says that 60 per cent of youth prioritise jobs over relationships.[30]

The Loneliness Tax

Here's the dark truth: The top of the mountain is lonely. Not because others couldn't climb but because we burnt every bridge on our way up. That's not success. That's expensive loneliness.

Daadi maa didn't need Harvard. But she knew that close relationships add ten years to our life. That's not friendship. That's life insurance with hugs.

In my lowest moments, I didn't survive because I was strong. I survived because I was held. By my sisters, my best friend Megha, my nieces Lehar and Navya. They didn't fix things. They just didn't leave. Sometimes, love is not loud. It's just there.

We confuse silence with strength. You smile. You show up. But inside, you're carrying a mountain. If that's you, I get it. You're not weak. You're tired. Maybe it's time to let someone in. Even superheroes need a couch and a hug.

Here's a stat you can't ignore: loneliness hits your body like fifteen cigarettes a day, according to a research article by American psychologist J. Holt-Lunstad.[31] You're not alone. You're just … unplugged. We have replaced hugs with likes. Heart-to-hearts with memes. We know what our friends ate today. But not what's eating them.

When my father passed away, I wasn't ready. I had things to say. That I was proud to be his son. That I missed how he always put me first. But life didn't wait. One day he was there, and the next he was gone. One moment you're arguing about something trivial and the next … the chair is empty.

Don't wait. Say the damn thing. Don't let ego write a story you'll spend a lifetime regretting. Some people would trade everything for one more hug. One more awkward 'I miss you'. But they can't. That moment's gone. Don't let 'someday' become 'too late'. You don't need 500 followers. You need five people who'll show up at 2 a.m.

What About Solitude?

Solitude is way better than relationships that aren't good for us. But solitude isn't loneliness. It's not a bug in your system that needs fixing. Solitude is a love affair with existence. It's enjoying your own company. It's the silence in where you feel God's breath. It's the space where you stop begging for likes and start listening to your own heartbeat.

There are three types of relationships: with others, with yourself, and with the Supreme Power (if you believe in one). The first one isn't always in your control. People come and go. Sometimes they stay, sometimes they don't. But the other two? They're your foundation. There's no substitute for them.

If solitude gives you peace, power and clarity, then own it. That's your design. If it makes you restless or hollow, maybe it's a nudge to reconnect. Not just with people, but with yourself … and with something bigger than you. Because here's the truth: being alone isn't the problem. Being disconnected—from self, from God, from love—is real poverty. You can chase millions. But you'll only miss the ones who stayed for free. And the shortcut for that? Give love first.

Do the Damn Thing: Strengthen Your Circle

Reflect: Who are the top three people who matter most to you right now?

Act: Pick one. Call them. Write a poem. Or just land up with biryani. Connection > caption.

14

Stop Waiting. Start Loving.

'A bit of fragrance always clings to the hand that gives you roses.'
—Chinese Proverb

'I'm unhappy because XYZ didn't love me.
Also because they saw my story and didn't reply.
Clearly, I deserve therapy … and a Nobel Prize for not slapping them.'

Sounds familiar? We've all said it. Maybe not out loud. But definitely in our overthinking, over-dramatic brains.

We wait. For affection. For replies. For appreciation. And when it doesn't come? We shrink. Sulk. Spiral. Convince ourselves we're unlovable.

But what if the equation is reversed? What if the love we're dying to receive … is the love we were born to give?

The Three-Month Experiment That Brought Love Back

In 2017, my life looked sorted on the outside. Inside? I was numb. My marriage was crumbling. I cracked jokes with friends, then came home to an emptiness so loud that even Alexa stayed quiet.

So I flipped the script. I stopped waiting to be loved. And started giving love. Unconditionally. Relentlessly. Even awkwardly. For three months, I set two rules:

- Make one person smile. It could be a compliment, a message or a gift, even if it was a meme.
- Speak to someone new—even if it was just 'Hi, bhaiya' to the building guard.

I complimented strangers. Helped blind/old people cross roads. Messaged forgotten friends. Wished employees I barely knew. One even said, 'Which Vishnu?' and hung up after I called him. My ego had left the group.

But slowly … something shifted. Not in them but in me. The more love I gave, the more whole I felt. Not because others gave it back but because I stopped needing them to.

Stand-up comedian Zakir Khan puts it beautifully: 'Life feels light when you give more to your people—love, help, money, even small gifts. But it feels heavy when you start expecting or taking more than you give.' Simple. Profound. True.

You don't get love by begging. You generate it—by living like love is already yours. That energy is magnetic. It changes you. And when you change, your reality shifts—even if no one else moves a muscle.

Class 6. No English. No Voice. No Friends

I was sent to a boarding school in sixth standard. Staying away from home is scary enough for any kid. Mine was an English-medium school—and I didn't speak a single word of the language.

Kids mocked my silence. 'You people from Bihar do not deserve to study. You're spoiling the vibe.' I felt invisible. Dumb. Disposable.

Then one day there was a surprise twist. My name got called out in assembly; I had topped my class. The kid who hadn't spoken to anyone in weeks had quietly outranked the rest. The boys who mocked me apologised, and soon became my friends.

Lesson: I only focused on myself. And my world changed.

We want the world to adjust to our whims. 'My partner should be more sensitive.' 'My parents should evolve.' 'My boss should have a soul.' But life doesn't change on demand. You do. And when you change—your vibe, your energy, your standards—something strange happens: people around you start behaving differently. Or they don't ... and you stop caring.

You don't need to fix the whole world. Just light your own damn lamp. Or at the very least, stop blowing out everyone else's.

Sadhguru puts it bluntly: 'If you're expecting someone else to make you happy, you're already on the path to misery.'

Give love—even when it's not returned. Grow—even when no one claps at your achievements. Forgive—even when they don't deserve it. Waiting for others to change is like waiting for your ex to apologise with emotional maturity. It's unlikely, painful and not worth the wait. But changing yourself? That's freedom. That's peace without permission.

Do the Damn Thing: Start with the Mirror

Reflect: What part of your life are you outsourcing to someone else's behaviour?

Act: What would shift if *you* changed your attitude, response and energy first? Take the step today.

15

Buddha Says Chill. Rocky Says Fight

'When you realise nothing is lacking, the whole world belongs to you.'

—*Lao Tzu*

Reel 1: A spiritual guru whispers:

'Love yourself. You are already whole. Accept everything.'

Reel 2: A motivational guru screams:

'Push harder! You are NOT enough! Hustle, grind, suffer, WIN!'

Both have millions of views. And you? You're brushing your teeth, stuck between enlightenment and Excel sheets.

Do you meditate … or dominate? Should you sit in silence? Or chase that next big win? Do you need healing or hustling? Whom do you follow?

Good news: They are not saying two different things. You can choose both. You don't have to choose between 'I'm enough' and 'I want more.' You can be both.

Self-Love Is Savage

Raj and Khushi both wanted to lose 15 kilos.

Raj hated his body. Every time he saw himself in the mirror, he cringed. 'I need to change this,' he thought. 'I can't live like this.'

Khushi, on the other hand, loved her body. She didn't want to fix it—she wanted to honour it. Her goal wasn't punishment. It was care.

They both lost 5 kilos within 2 months. Raj felt … less disgusted and relieved. And less motivated. Khushi felt proud, energised—and even more connected to herself.

Guess who stuck with it? Guess who enjoyed the journey more? Obviously, Khushi.

Because hatred might get you started. But only love makes you stay.

Don't try to change yourself because you hate yourself. Do it because you love yourself. Deeply. Fiercely. Unapologetically.

Raj ran on guilt like a cheap diesel engine—loud and toxic—and eventually he broke down. Khushi ran on love—smooth, sustainable and plenty of mileage.

When you truly love someone—you want the best for them. Why should it be any different for you?

I once heard Sachin Tendulkar say after missing a century: 'I'm happy, but not satisfied.' He gave his best—and still believed he could improve. Not because he hated himself. But because he respected his craft.

You can be proud and want more. Real growth doesn't need self-hate. It needs self-honesty. And self-love.

Take Serena Williams. One of the greatest athletes ever. But after a tough loss, she once said: 'I always believe I can beat the best. But I also forgive myself when I fall.' She didn't become great by hating herself. She did so by respecting her journey. That's not weakness. That's power.

Think of a toddler learning to walk. They fall ten times. No one yells: 'Walk properly, idiot.' But that's how we talk to ourselves every Monday.

You are not broken. You don't need fixing. You need nurturing. You need an update.

Self-Love Isn't the End. It's the Engine

Reel 3: The hero stares at both gurus … and presses *Mute*. Then creates his own reel. One where the hero is kind … and powerful. Where growth doesn't come from shame but from love.

Because the world has enough critics. What it needs is one more hero who actually cares about themselves. Because self-love isn't the end of growth. It's where real growth finally begins.

Do the Damn Thing: Show Yourself Some Love

Reflect: What's one thing you've been harsh on yourself about lately?

Act: Write a short, kind message to yourself—as if you were comforting a close friend—and read it every morning for the next seven days. You don't need to change to be loved. But once you love yourself, change becomes inevitable.

Bonus: The Happiness Audit

Rate each statement mentioned below from 1 to 5 (1 = Never, 5 = Always). Be honest—this is for your personal reflection!

1. Brain Chemistry Boosters

- ☐ I engage in activities that give me a sense of achievement. *(Dopamine)*
- ☐ I spend time outdoors or move my body daily. *(Serotonin & endorphins)*
- ☐ I laugh often and engage in activities that bring me joy. *(Endorphins)*
- ☐ I have deep, meaningful conversations with people I care about. *(Oxytocin)*

2. Daily Happiness Habits

- ☐ I exercise regularly, even if it's just a walk.
- ☐ I eat a balanced diet that supports my energy and mood.
- ☐ I get enough sleep and wake up feeling rested.
- ☐ I take breaks from screens and social media.

3. Emotional Well-being

- ☐ I focus on what I can control and let go of what I can't.
- ☐ I practise gratitude by focusing on the good in my life.
- ☐ I challenge negative thoughts and shift my perspective.
- ☐ I forgive myself and others instead of holding on to resentment.

4. Relationships and Connection

- ☐ I spend quality time with friends and family.
- ☐ I express appreciation and kindness to others.
- ☐ I feel a sense of belonging in my social circles.
- ☐ I ask for help or support when I need it.

5. Personal Growth and Self-Acceptance

- ☐ I take time out for hobbies or activities that bring me joy.
- ☐ I set personal goals and actively work towards them.
- ☐ I make decisions based on what I want, not just to please others.
- ☐ I feel comfortable being my authentic self.

6. Living in the Moment

- ☐ I take time to enjoy small moments instead of rushing through life.
- ☐ I engage in activities that make me feel 'in the zone'.
- ☐ I practise mindfulness or meditation, even in simple ways.
- ☐ I limit multitasking and focus on being present.

Your Score and Reflection

- **100+ points:** You're actively creating happiness in your life! Keep it up.
- **70–99 points:** You're doing well, but there's room for improvement.
- **50–69 points:** You may need to focus on specific areas of happiness—pick **two or three habits** to work on.
- **Below 50 points:** Time to make a change! Start with small steps from the checklist above.

Good job!

The questions you answered are not just for reflection but for your personal transformation. Small, conscious changes in your daily life can create a lasting impact. So, what's one step you will take today towards a happier life? Remember, happiness starts with you. Choose it, nurture it and let it grow.

SECTION 2

SUCCESS

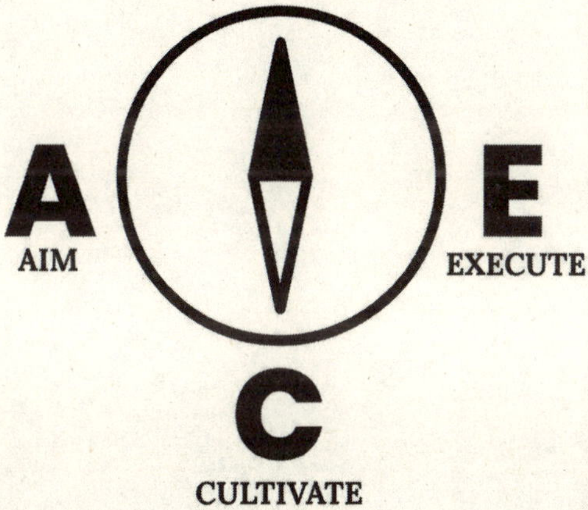

Inspired by Lord Narsingh

Hiranyakashipu, the demon king, was invincible—or so he thought. No man or animal could kill him. Not inside, not outside. Not during the day, not at night. Not by weapon, not by hand.

Vishnu appeared as Narsingh—half-man, half-lion—at twilight (not day, not night), on the threshold (not inside, not outside) and tore him apart with claws (not a weapon, not a hand).

Lesson: When the problem exists because of rules, you fight smarter and change the rules themselves.

16

Don't Chase the Label. Chase the Damn Feeling

'If you don't know where you are going, any road will take you there.'

—Lewis Carroll in Alice in Wonderland *(Also every confused twenty-something on LinkedIn)*

In 2007, I was in my final year at IIM Ahmedabad. Everyone was chasing the same thing—big brand, bigger salary, global office, a buzzword life. I could've joined the race, but something inside me kept whispering: *'Is this your dream—or just society's Pinterest board?'*

I didn't have a five-year plan. Hell, I didn't even have a five-week one. No idea. No capital. No connections. Just one weird, stubborn desire: *'Build something of my own.'*

So I did the unthinkable. I said NO to a ₹1-crore international investment banking job and took a smaller role to work on my business plan. Was I scared? You bet! But I whispered to myself like a B-grade Bollywood hero: *'Dar ke aage . . . jeet hai.'*

On the last day of college, a TV anchor who had come to cover the placements asked me: 'What's the best part about graduating from IIM-A? The crore package?' I smiled and said: 'No. It's that someone like me could say NO to it.' That moment made me feel free—free from chasing someone else's idea of success. I was happy knowing that even if I failed, I would fail living my dream and not someone else's.

First Principle, Boss! Why Fun > Force

Your brain runs on one ancient rule: chase pleasure and avoid pain. So when your work feels like punishment, you'll resist it—consciously or subconsciously.

But when it feels like *play*, dopamine flows. You lose track of time. You *want* to come back to the office tomorrow. That's why consistency beats talent. That's why people who enjoy their work don't just survive—they dominate.

Follow Your Dharma

Every one of us is wired differently. But society loves pressing *copy-paste*. Trends. Rat races. 'Safe' careers. It's a factory that makes people average by making them chase labels. But that's like buying shoes two sizes small because they're trending. Sure, they look good on Instagram. But walk a mile in them and you'll bleed.

Judge a fish by its ability to climb a tree and it'll spend life thinking it's useless. Judge singer Arijit Singh on how many sixes he can hit and—well, good luck. We're all born with a dharma—a thing we're meant to do. A game we're naturally good at.

But that plan is not always obvious. Sometimes your 'inner voice' is just … buffering. And that's okay. There's no expiry date stamped on your soul. Take your time. Experiment. Just ask yourself: what work makes me forget to check my phone? What problems do I secretly want to fix? What am I better at than most people? And, yes, what the world will actually pay me for. The Japanese have a word for this: *Ikigai*.[32]

A 2023 LinkedIn India report shows many Gen Z feel stuck in dead-end jobs.[33] Do you know why? Because most people don't follow goals. They follow labels. Safe, fancy-sounding ones. But not the ones that make them feel alive.

Great people listen to their hearts and take risks. Take, for instance, the Kamath brothers. Nikhil dropped out of school at sixteen. Nithin took customer service calls to fund his stock trading. No IIM education. No pitch decks. Just one thing: clarity. While the world chased unicorn labels, they quietly built Zerodha—India's largest stockbroker. Zero funding. Zero fluff. Full heart.

Success isn't about what impresses others. It's about what obsesses you.

Write the Damn Thing Down

Once the whisper shows up, capture it. Because dreams that stay in your head turn into noise. Studies say you're 42 per cent more likely to achieve a goal if you write it down.[34]

So write it down. Stick it on your fridge. Frame it like it's your firstborn. Don't make a list of twenty-seven goals. Start with one. Make it S.M.A.R.T.

- **Specific:** '*Work out 3x a week.*'
- **Measurable:** '*Save ₹5,000/month.*'

- **Attainable + Realistic:** Push yourself, but don't audition for *Avengers*.
- **Time-bound:** Because 'someday' is code for 'never'.

If your dream feels exciting—and a little terrifying—that's the one for you. Because one honest step towards your dream is worth more than a lifetime of sprinting towards someone else's.

You've just found your destination. Now the real question is: Are you dreaming big enough—or just safe enough? Let's find out in the next chapter.

Do the Damn Thing: Set Your GPS

Reflect: What's one goal that actually excites you?

Act: Make it S.M.A.R.T. Write it down, add a deadline and move.

17

Dream Like a Psycho. Work Like You're Not

'What a man thinks, he becomes.'

—Maitri Upanishad

(Also every entrepreneur's screensaver)

In my hostel room one night, my brain was marinating in self-doubt. It was 2:04 a.m., and I was wide awake. That's when my roommate Abhishek asked, 'What's your plan after college?' I mumbled, 'Maybe an MBA ...' He asked, 'Where?' I replied, 'Any decent one. Not the IIMs or anything crazy.'

He stared at me: 'Why not the IIMs?' I laughed. 'Bro, please. I can't even speak English properly. IIMs are for toppers with Google internships.' Then he said something that cracked my skull open:

'Don't park your Ferrari in a garage just because you're scared of traffic.'

Step 1: Dream Big

You're not scared of failing. You're scared of looking stupid. So you shrink your dreams, play it safe. And one day, you wake up in a LinkedIn-friendly life that feels nothing like you. Meanwhile, someone with half your talent is out there winning. Why? Because they dared to dream big.

It's like the classic flea-in-a-jar metaphor: fleas were trapped in a jar, but they kept flying around and hitting the lid. Eventually, they stopped trying. Even when the lid was removed, they still jumped low. The ceiling was gone, but their belief stayed broken. That's what life does. Critics and rejections don't kill the dream; they kill the jump.

But hey, why this pressure to 'dream big'?

Not everyone wants to build a unicorn, climb Mount Everest or become India's Elon Musk. And that's okay. Some people just want a peaceful home, a job they enjoy, a few real friends and time for evening chai. That's not mediocrity. That's clarity.

Who decides what's 'big', anyway? For one person, it's scaling a start-up. For another, it's healing their body. Or raising a kind child. Or learning how to sleep without anxiety.

Don't let society's scoreboard hijack your soul's desires. If your heart lights up at simple goals—honour them. Peace is a flex too. But ... if you're one of the cursed ones—if you can't stop thinking bigger, if your gut keeps whispering, 'There's more for you'—then you owe it to yourself to give it your all. Say the scary goal out loud. And chase it with irrational, beautiful madness.

Step 2: Visualise Your Success

We were a small start-up about to sign on Malaika Arora—fit, famous, affordable. Then my 'never-satisfied' brain whispered:

'Forget the budget. Who's the dream pick?' Answer: 'Aishwarya Rai Bachchan.' She wasn't just a fit—she was a flex. A global icon, working mom and a public transformation story.

The problem was that we had a budget for a bicycle. And she was a Rolls Royce. Worse—we wanted her to endorse *and* invest. (Marwaris don't just dream big, we send the invoice too.)

Our marketing agency laughed. 'Are you crazy? She's out of reach. Don't even try.' That 'no' was enough fuel. I went home and printed two mock ads with her face—one for my home, one for the office. I stared at them daily—maybe more than my ex (explains the break-up).

And then I chased it. Follow-ups. Meetings. Rejections. I treated it like a college crush, and months later she said yes. Not just as a face but as an investor.

Was it just luck? Maybe. But I believe it was something else: visualisation, backed by massive follow-ups and start-up-grade delusion.

Step 3: Act

'Just visualise and it'll come true.' Yeah, right! By that logic, we'd all have Hrithik Roshan abs and Bill Gates's bank balance. Visualisation works because you do.

Will it always work? Hell, no. I've visualised things that never happened. Visualisation isn't a guarantee. It's a multiplier. It takes your odds from 10 per cent to 30 per cent, maybe even 50 per cent. Sometimes, that's all you need.

The Paradox Nobody Talks About

Western self-help screams: 'Manifest it. Own it. Work till it bends.' And truth is, that works—sometimes. But Eastern wisdom whispers a different hack: 'Do your karma. Forget about the phal.' Dream, hustle, visualise, act—but then let go.

Is that a contradiction? Nope. It's a survival strategy. Without Western drive, you'll never stretch for the impossible. Without Eastern surrender, you'll lose your mind when it doesn't pan out. Put another way: **West:** Control is power. **East:** Letting go is power. The real cheat code? Both.

Dream like a psycho. Work like you're not. And surrender like a saint.

Unlock Your Mahi

A lot of people advise others to be realistic. That is quite a scam. Realistic people don't change the world. They file paperwork. They adjust dreams to fit spreadsheets.

What if M.S. Dhoni had stayed a ticket checker? The world would've missed the helicopter shot. So here's your script: dream wild, deliver clean. Say the crazy thing out loud. Take one scary step. Repeat.

Your Ferrari's waiting. Don't keep it parked forever. Move—or AI will drive it away.

Do the Damn Thing: Put Your Dream on Display

Reflect: What does your dream *look and feel* like?

Act: Create a vision board. Use real images. Stick it where you'll see it daily. And then? Back it up with moves. Not just mantras.

18

When the Cheese Moves, Move Your Ass

'It is not the strongest or the smartest who survive, but the ones most adaptable to change.'

—Charles Darwin

In 1975, a young engineer at Kodak built the world's first digital camera. He showed it to his bosses. They smiled and said, 'Nice. But who would ever want to see photos on a screen?' Kodak had the future in its hands. They even filed a patent—but locked it away. Why? Because film was making them too much money. They didn't want to change. Years later, Sony, Canon and Apple took over. Kodak went bankrupt. It's the same story with Blackberry. They thought smartphones were toys.

The lesson here is that if you don't change when the world changes, you disappear—even if you saw it coming.

Loss = Leverage

There are two types of people who must read the book *Who Moved My Cheese?*. People who love reading and people who hate reading. It's the easiest book you'll ever read—thirty minutes, maybe less. But the lesson? That's a big one.

When your cheese is gone, don't cry. Find new cheese. Maybe it's bigger. Maybe it's better. It's simple advice, but most people don't follow it. They hold on to old jobs, dreams and comfort zones, as if nothing has changed. Spoiler: everything has. Adapt. Or disappear.

A 2023 MIT-affiliated study found that between 47 and 56 per cent of all tasks could be at least partially automated with large-language-model software.[35] Not 'someday'. Now. Ten coders shrink to one coder plus ten great prompts. Feel the panic? Good! Panic is data. Panic means you're awake.

Sure, it's scary. But it's also a blessing in disguise. Sometimes it takes a big bully like AI to kick you out of your comfort zone—and push you towards a better life. No more boring, soul-sucking jobs. You'll be forced to upgrade. Learn faster. Think sharper. Create better. With the right skills, you'll do work that actually matters. Ten times the output. Ten times the joy. That's not a threat. That's an upgrade. AI doesn't want your job. It wants your boring tasks. So you can finally stop pretending *copy-paste* was your life's mission.

Researchers call it the Productivity J-Curve: tech kills routine jobs first, then creates more roles, more pay and more possibilities—for those who reskill early. Change looks like loss before it feels like leverage.

Upgrade Mode: Ninety-Day Survival Kit

1. *Audit the cheese.* List your weekly tasks. Highlight anything repeatable or boring. That's tomorrow's AI breakfast.
2. *Pick a power skill.* Creativity, storytelling, persuasive communication, strategic thinking—stuff algorithms still fumble with.
3. *Co-pilot with bots.* Strap on AI like Iron Man's suit.
4. *Build a public sandbox.* Share your learning—threads, reels, newsletters. Visibility = luck. Luck = opportunities.
5. *Schedule quarterly upgrades.* Learn a new tool, invest in a new course, build a new contact. Autopilot growth > panic growth.

Remember: extinction isn't an event. It's a delay—in learning, adapting or letting go of the 9-to-5 cheese you thought was forever.

Mic Drop: Ride the Bully

If one person can now do the job of ten—what do the other nine do? It's simple: evolve. Humans always have. Cars. Computers. Machines. Yes, they killed some jobs. But they created millions more—and made life better. Today, the average person lives better than kings 200 years ago. TVs. Hot showers. Ice cream on demand.

AI will push that even further. Flying cars, 100-year lifespans, four-hour workdays. Sounds wild? Maybe. But it's possible—if you're willing to adapt. So sniff often. Move early. Change is a bully—until you ride its shoulders.

19

Fixed Is Fiction. Grow the Hell Up

'Whether you think you can or you think you can't—you're right.'

—Henry Ford

Let me tell you the most dangerous drug on the planet. Not weed. Not sugar. Not even Instagram likes. It's comfort. Comfort feels harmless and nice. Until one day you realise that it's been five years since you did something that scared you. What you need a little more in your life isn't more motivation but more embarrassment. Confidence doesn't come first. It comes limping in—after ten cringe attempts and one accidental viral video. Want proof? Read on.

From 'Happy Birthday Text Guy' to Insta Video Guy

I dislike cameras more than karela. I prefer not to be in front of one. My will to live was tested when I had to record a video wishing a friend on his birthday. It was supposed to be just five seconds long. But I took seventeen takes. And in the end, I still deleted all of them. And ended up texting: 'HBD. Stay blessed :)' instead.

I felt small in front of the camera. Like my voice didn't deserve to be heard. But deep down I knew I had something to say. I wanted to help people live healthier lives. And that meant facing the lens.

So I joined a public speaking course. And I hated every second. I forgot lines. I stammered. I once said 'nutritional intercourse' instead of 'intervention'. Kill me.

But I kept showing up. Cringing and retrying. Until one day—I didn't cringe. I spoke. And people listened. Today, I talk to millions online. On video. With comfort. Now I know that confidence doesn't come first. Reps do. Now let's see where your mindset stands.

Quick Mindset Check

1. When I fail at something …
   A. I avoid trying again.
   B. I try to learn from it.
2. When I see someone doing better than me …
   A. I feel insecure.
   B. I feel inspired (and maybe stalk their LinkedIn profile a little).
3. When someone gives me feedback …
   A. I feel judged and defensive.
   B. I nod, take notes, and secretly cry later (kidding … sort of).
4. Intelligence is …
   A. Mostly fixed.

B. Grown with practice (and lots of Google searches).

5. I love things that …

A. Come naturally and don't make me sweat.

B. Challenge me and make me question all my life choices (in a good way).

If you've chosen mostly As, you're not broken. You're just running on old software. It's time for an update.

Mostly Bs? You're already flexing that growth mindset. Keep lifting.

First Principle, Boss! Why Growth Feels Like Sh*t

Change = threat. Comfort = safety.

That's why growth feels like panic, not progress. But here's the deal:

You only grow by breaking what's holding you back. It hurts—but so does staying stuck.

You're Not Wired. You're Trainable

In Dweck's research, students who were taught a growth mindset showed measurable improvements in academic performance, especially in maths.[36] Why? Not because their IQ changed. Their beliefs had. Even brain scans prove this—your brain literally rewires when you stretch it. That's called neuroplasticity.[37]

Your mindset isn't set in cement. It's like clay, which shapes with effort. Have you ever seen a goldfish in one of those small plastic bags from the pet shop? Even when you drop it into a giant aquarium, it still circles that same tiny corner. Why? Because it's still swimming in the memory of a plastic bag.

That's what most of us do. We keep swimming a short distance—even when the tank is huge. But nothing legendary happens in the comfort zone.

Growth is like a snake shedding skin—uncomfortable and vulnerable. But if it doesn't shed, it suffocates. Comfort feels safe—until it chokes you. What if the thing you're most scared to try … is exactly the thing that will change your life? Go there. Mess up. Laugh. Grow.

Up next: Your growth depends on one more brutal question—who's really in control? The next chapter hands you back the keys.

Do the Damn Thing: Reinvent Yourself

Reflect: What's one label you've worn that doesn't fit anymore? Maybe it's 'shy', 'not creative' or 'bad with numbers'.

Act: This week, do one thing your old self would've never dared to. Do it messy, but do it anyway. That's how reinvention begins.

20

The Control Illusion: Who's Really Driving?

'Some things are in our control and others not.'

—Epictetus

(aka ancient Greek Gaur Gopal Das)

When Wilma Rudolph was four, polio wrecked her leg. Doctors said she may never walk again. Most people would've taken that diagnosis, added sad music and given up. But not Wilma. She didn't have a rich dad, fancy doctors or a grand plan. She just learnt to walk. And then run. And then? She won three Olympic golds—in sprinting.

It was the same world with its chaos as before. But Wilma didn't wait for a miracle. She became one.

Which brings us to you: who's really running your life—you or your excuses?

Quick Reality Check: Who's Behind the Wheel?

What sounds more like you?

1. When I fail …
   A. I look for what I can learn.
   B. I assume it wasn't meant to be.
2. My life will improve when …
   A. I make different choices.
   B. The universe finally stops ghosting me.
3. Success depends mostly on …
   A. My effort and habits.
   B. Luck, timing, the evil eye and Mercury retrograde.
4. When I see someone crushing it …
   A. I admire their grind.
   B. I lowkey think they just got lucky.

Mostly As? You're driving.

Mostly Bs? You're waiting for Uber Destiny.

Psychologists call this **locus of control**.[38] It's a fancy term for a simple idea.

- Internal locus: I create my life.
- External locus: Life just happens to me.

The Paradox: West vs East

Here's where it gets spicy.

- Western philosophy: Own everything. You're in charge. It heavily leans towards internal locus.

- Eastern philosophy. Do your karma. Results aren't yours. Surrender them to God. It's largely an external locus.

The sweet spot is both: Act like a hustler. Chill like a yogi.

Because pure internal locus without surrender may lead to arrogance and burnout. And pure surrender without action = passivity + victimhood.

I believe in destiny. I also believe in karma. You may think that's a contradiction, but it's really not. Your actions are in your hands. The outcomes are not.

Sometimes karma pays off, sometimes it doesn't. That doesn't mean effort is pointless—it just means you're human, not a god. Even Krishna, the OG life coach, said the same.

Our texts didn't glorify bhagya (fate). They spoke about prārabdha—past karma unfolding. But even that needs action in the present moment to activate it. Without karma, even destiny just sits on the couch scrolling Reels.

So no, you can't control the storm. But you can adjust the sails. And that single shift—'This is on me'—turns you from a passenger into the pilot.

However, not everyone starts from the same line. Some people are born into storms—caste, class, gender, history. Luck is uneven. As Harari reminds us, you're not just your choices. You're also biology + history.[39] But here's the cheat code: balance your locus. External helps you accept. Internal helps you improve.

Mic Drop: How to Snatch the Wheel Back

Not everything's your fault. Not everything's out of your hands either. Instead of asking 'Why me?', ask 'What now?'

- *Focus on what's yours*: Make two lists:
  – Can't control: weather, traffic, exes
  – Can control: actions, attitude, playlist

Burn the first. Frame the second.

- *Win small, win fast*: Don't wait to change everything. Just win today. Make your bed. Walk for ten minutes. Skip one soda drink. Your brain loves proof. Feed it. Act before you're ready, especially since nobody ever feels 'ready'.

Start. Suck. Learn. Repeat.

- *Victim or hero? Pick one*: Blaming is easy. 'My boss is toxic.' 'My childhood was hard.' But here's the truth: you can write the world's longest complaint list. Or you can rewrite your script. You can't do both.

Up next: Motivation is a scam. Here's what works instead.

Do the Damn Thing: The Control Shift

Reflect: Think of a recent L you took. *(For non-Gen Z folks: L = Loss, not Love or Lassi.)* Be brutally honest—did you blame something or own it?

Act: Name *one thing* you could've done differently. Then go do *that* next time. No excuses. No drama. Just drive.

21

Motivation is Overrated. Try These Two Brutal Tricks Instead

'Discipline weighs ounces. Regret weighs tons.'

—Jim Rohn

Motivation is like your memory when the teacher suddenly asks you a question in class. It's there all the time—until you actually need it. Then poof! It's gone. Motivation is the biggest scam when it comes to self-help. I'm about to give you two brutal tricks that beat motivation every damn time.

Trick #1: Make Short-Term Pain > Short-Term Pleasure

Back in the day, a Marwari friend and I were trying to quit smoking. We tried it all: guilt, gums and 'this is my last one' lies. But at ₹10 a stick, there was no pain. So I made a rule: smoke a cigarette = pay ₹500. Not to the government. Not to charity. To each other.

That was it. The lungs still said yes. But the wallets screamed, 'NOPE.' Suddenly, the short-term joy came with short-term pain. And nothing terrifies a Marwari more than non-refundable cash loss.

This isn't just desi jugaad. I heard of this guy who scheduled an automatic tweet for 6:10 a.m. every day: 'I'm lazy and couldn't wake up. Reply and I'll PayPal you $5.' If he didn't get up and stop it in time, the tweet would go out to the world—and he'd have to pay strangers. Imagine sleeping in and waking up to 100 DMs saying, 'Where's my $5?' It's safe to say, he became a morning person real fast.[40]

He didn't need motivation. He needed consequences. Here's the truth bomb for why this strategy works: your brain isn't built for long-term success. It's built for short-term pleasure and pain avoidance. Most good habits = short-term pain. Most bad habits = instant dopamine.

Want to win in life? You've got to flip that equation. Want to wake up at 6 a.m.? Miss it = donate your favourite hoodie. Still miss it? Cut your partner's favourite hoodie into two. Now we're playing serious games. It works for anything. Junk binge? No phone for twenty-four hours. Skip studies? Wash every dish in the sink—even your flatmate's.

Trick #2: The Draupadi Challenge

Draupadi stood there, hair loose, eyes blazing—and made a vow: 'I will not tie my hair until Duryodhan is destroyed.' It drove five warriors, a kingdom and eighteen days of epic war to make it happen. That's the power of a personal vow. A Draupadi Challenge.

Inspired, I made mine. I gave up my absolute soul-fix: badminton. Not forever—just until my abs showed up. No more shuttle, sweat or the post-smash dopamine hit. It felt like breaking up with joy. But that ache turned into fuel. That sacrifice created an obsession. Suddenly, six-packs didn't feel like 'motivation'. They felt like a mission.

In the movie *Chhichhore*, each misfit gave up something they loved. One quit swearing. One quit smoking. One quit porn. One gave up his girlfriend. Why? Not to be saints. But to build grit. Sacrifice → Obsession → Momentum → Habit. That's how legends are built.

If It Doesn't Hurt, It Won't Work

When you attach pain to failure and purpose to sacrifice, great things can happen. Dreams don't die because they are impossible. They die because you didn't bleed for them. (Not literally—unless you're boxing.) Don't ask: 'Do I want it?' Ask: 'What am I willing to give up for it?' Short-term pain now … or long-term regret forever? Pick your fighter.

You've learnt discipline. Now use it to upgrade—or get killed by AI in cold algorithmic blood.

22

Learn Fast. Unlearn Faster

'Once you stop learning, you start dying.'

—Albert Einstein
(a man who never had a bad hair day)

If Elon Musk gave you one day to teach his life lessons, what would it cost? ₹4,500 crore. (That's how much he earned per day in 2024.) But here's the hack: you can rent his brain for ₹499. You just need to read his biography.

Books = time travel without a passport. You skip their heartbreak. You steal their secrets. And you fast-forward your own growth. Why wait for life to slap you? Pick up a damn book. Upgrade without the bruises.

AI Is Coming After You. Are You Prepared?

AI reads 1,000 books while you finish a reel. And you? Still resisting feedback from three people. Still clinging to outdated ideas like they're ancestral property. Bruh, you're not competing with your cousin anymore. You're in a race with machines. And the machine doesn't sleep, sulk or Netflix.

You want to stay in the game? Stay curious. Stay light. Stay update-able. You're either Version 10.2—or you're the floppy disk of your industry. The good news is that AI can write code. But it can't feel emotions or have gut instinct. That's your edge—if you learn how to use it.

'But I Hate Reading ...'

So what? I hate squats, but I still do them. Because I like knees that work. Winners don't just do what they love. They do what's needed. Most people wait to 'feel like learning'. That's why they're still bingeing reels on how to get rich.

A study showed that 85 per cent of self-made millionaires read more than two books a month.[41] Coincidence? No way. It's just compound interest—for your brain.

If you don't like reading, you can always mix it up.

- *Mentors and coaches*: One good mentor can save you five bad years.
- *Experiences*: Courses, workshops, even that expensive Tony Robbins event I flew to Singapore for. It cost me ₹1.5 lakh—and my ego. But my mindset? It definitely got an upgrade.
- *Stories everywhere*: Biopics, podcasts, audiobooks, movies. Stories teach what lectures can't—your heart remembers what your head forgets.

Ancient India Was Already Doing This

Saraswati holds a book, not a gold chain. She plays the veena, not crypto. And Lakshmi follows Saraswati—not the other way around. What does that mean? Wisdom first. Wealth later. You chase knowledge, and life chases you. You chase money, and anxiety chases you.

People often ask me how I survived fifty days in jail. It was just me and my books. One a day. Sometimes two. I turned my cell into a Think Week (inspired by Bill Gates). He had a lake for his retreat. I had a leaky ceiling. It still worked. And somewhere in that silence, this book was born. On my forty-ninth day in jail, the idea for this book came alive. As if God was saying, 'Lesson learnt—now you're free.' The darkest phase of my life gave me the brightest gift I've ever created. My pain turned into my purpose. And it started with reading and learning.

In the age of AI, learning is not a hobby. It's your oxygen mask. Learn fast and execute faster.

Exercise: Your Learning Plan

Reflect: What's one new thing you want to learn in the next three months?

Act: How will you learn it—books, courses, mentors or workshops? Allocate time and a budget for it. Because learning is the only investment that never crashes.

23

Version One > Version None

'If you wait for perfect, you'll wait forever. And then die.'
—Ancient Indian auntie (probably)

'Once I find the perfect idea …' 'Once this design is perfect …'

Sound familiar? Perfectionism is the classic trap. It wears ambition like a mask, but underneath it's just fear in a tuxedo. The truth is that perfection has killed more dreams than failure ever could. Perfection is the reason why your podcast, reel, start-up or speech is still chilling in drafts.

Version one beats waiting for perfection every time. Research from the University of Bath links perfectionism to burnout, depression and the saddest death of all: waiting.[42] But the idea of perfection is a scam. Even Steve Jobs didn't wait for perfect. The first iPhone had no copy-paste option, no App Store and no front camera. It still changed the world. If he'd waited for perfect, we'd still be playing Snake on a Nokia 1100. Sometimes, *'good enough'* is genius enough.

When I started my nutrition business, I had no funding, no subject knowledge and no investor support. So I read books, made products in my kitchen, packed them in silver foil—no brand, just vibes. I didn't even have ₹20K to pay the shopkeeper. He gave me credit. God bless him! I walked back holding a packet of hope in one hand—and crippling self-doubt in the other. That was my messy, stupid, imperfect beginning. But it worked. And we grew. A year later, we got funding. Lesson: Resourceful > Perfect.

But is perfection always bad? You can't ship a half-baked airplane. Or a pacemaker. Or code that powers bank servers. Some jobs need precision. So no—I'm not glorifying mediocrity. I just don't want you to let your obsession with perfection become an excuse for doing nothing. Polish later. But first, start. Let's do a simple test. Choose the option that best describes you:

1. A. It must be perfect, no matter how long.
   B. Progress is better than perfection.
2. A. I recheck work again and again.
   B. I check once or twice and move on.
3. A. If it's not 100 per cent, I redo it.
   B. It's good enough. Submit it.
4. A. I get stuck fearing it won't be perfect.
   B. I try anyway.
5. A. I redo others' work to perfect it.
   B. I trust others and move on.

Mostly As? Perfectionism may be holding you back.
Mostly Bs? You value excellence without getting stuck.

How to Escape the Perfect Trap

1. *Set a good enough deadline:* Timebox it. Then ship it.
2. *Ask better questions:* Not ‘*Is it perfect?*’ but ‘*Did I move today?*’
3. *Version One > Version None:* You’re not launching Chandrayaan (even though it *feels* like you are.)
4. *Create ugly. Polish later:* Inner critic not invited.
5. *Celebrate progress:* Don’t wait for results. Take action today.

‘But Aamir Khan is a perfectionist. And he is my favourite.’ I hear you. But even he pays the price. Blockbuster *Dangal* came in 2016. After that, he gave two massive flops. That’s nearly a decade with no hits—and a battle with depression. Also, he’s earned the right to obsess. You may be using ‘perfect’ to avoid starting. So here’s your only job today. Stutter. Stumble. Start anyway. Take the first messy step today. Even if it’s garbage. Especially if it’s garbage. Your future self is already clapping.

Up next: The 1 per cent that changes everything.

24

The 1-per-cent Advantage: Win by a Metre, Not a Mile

> *'The difference between ordinary and extraordinary is that little extra.'*
>
> —*Jimmy Johnson (American football coach)*

'I gave my 100 per cent.'

Buddy, no, you didn't. You gave 97 per cent. Maybe 98.5 per cent. Then you blamed the market, your ex, or fate. Here's the brutal truth: the last 1 per cent is where legends are made. The extra rep when your arms say no. One more email after twenty rejections. One last rehearsal when your brain screams, *'Chill, bro.'* It's not sexy, not Insta-worthy. But it's the difference between *'almost'* and *'I made it'*.

One Metre = One World Cup

Go back to the 2024 T20 World Cup Final. India vs South Africa. Last ball. Surya Kumar Yadav ran, leapt and caught the ball mid-air, millimetres from the rope. If that ball had gone even one metre further, it was game over for India. South Africa would've roared. One metre determined the winner.

Roger Federer. GOAT. Legend. You know what percentage of points he won in his entire career? *54 per cent.*[43] Just slightly better than average. But that tiny edge—repeated for decades—made him immortal. That's the 1 per cent rule.

But why do most people not give that last 1 per cent? Research shows the brain gets a dopamine hit before the goal is achieved—when we think we're close. That's why we often quit right before the finish line. We feel the high of progress and mistake it for completion. Don't trust the high. Trust the finish line.

Alibaba's Jack Ma got rejected by Harvard and KFC. Thomas Edison failed a thousand times before the lightbulb clicked. The moral of the story is that most people quit before the plot twist. But the greats wait for it—and rewrite the ending.

Take Colonel Sanders, for instance. At sixty-five, he was broke, and living off a $105 monthly pension. All he had was one fried chicken recipe and a dream. He travelled state to state in America, slept in his car and got rejected over 1,000 times while trying to franchise it. Most people would've stopped after ten rejections. Maybe fifty.

But the 1,009th time? Someone said yes, and the first Kentucky Fried Chicken franchise was born. This shows that you don't need everyone to believe in you. Just one person. But to get to that one, you have to survive the 1,008 before them.

You don't need to take big strides. Just being 1 per cent better every day is a great place to start. If you improve by 1 per cent a day, you're 37x better by the end of the year. Sounds like motivational BS? Okay, here's desi maths: run 1 km today. Add 50 metres daily. In three months, you'll run over 5 km. No steroids. No hype. Just compounding hustle.

The sad truth is that most dreams die at 99 per cent. Because you were tired. Because it was hard. Because you almost made it. But almost doesn't win titles.

So today, give your dream that extra 1 per cent. One more pitch. One more shot. One more try. Because the 1 per cent difference is what puts you in the top 1 per cent.

The finish line isn't far. It's just one tired, trembling step beyond where you usually stop. You've mastered the 1 per cent that adds up. Now let's talk about the stuff that needs to be cut out.

25

The Subtraction Superpower: Cut the Crap. Keep the Gold

'Perfection is achieved not when there is nothing more to add, but when there is nothing left to take away.'

—Antoine de Saint-Exupéry

In my second year at SRCC, I almost ran for general secretary of the student council. It was a big title, but deep down, I knew that if I said yes to this, I'd be saying no to CAT prep. Everyone said, 'Bro, you can manage both.' Which in college lingo means sleep for only four hours, pretend you're chilled and secretly cry into your Maggi.

I was tempted. Saying yes could've meant fame ... and maybe some extra attention from my crush (and her friends too). But I said no. I hated doing so because it felt like I was turning down my one shot at campus stardom. But that 'no' gave me focus. That focus gave me IIM Ahmedabad. And everything that came after.

That wasn't the only time I said no. During my MBA studies, I had the chance to choose a three-month exchange programme in Europe. Wine. Waffles. Eiffel Tower. It was everything a desi student dreams of. But I said no. Because I was writing my first book. While others made memories, I rewrote paragraphs. No Orkut. Just Microsoft Word. (Gen Z: Orkut was our dinosaur-era Instagram.) Was it boring? Yep. Was it worth it? Hell yes. Sometimes, saying no to Paris means saying yes to purpose.

Michelangelo to McDonald's—Everyone Follows This Secret

When asked how he sculpted *David*, Michelangelo said, 'I removed everything that wasn't David.' He didn't build greatness. He cut away everything that wasn't. That's subtraction. Less noise brought more clarity.

McDonald's once had a very long menu—until they realised that 80 per cent of sales came from just burgers, fries, beverages. So they cut the clutter and focused on what worked. And minted billions. You don't win by doing everything. You win by doing less better.

The Brain Loves Adding. But Greatness Comes from Subtracting

One of my college friends was studying for an M.Com degree, while prepping for CA, CS, Indian CFA, international CFA and MBA entrance exams. He was working night shifts at a consulting firm while selling insurance door to door during the day. I asked him, 'What do you actually want to do?' He said, 'IAS officer.' I had no words—at least none that can be printed. If multitasking was a degree, he'd have topped the class. But he would have probably missed convocation since he'd have been attending five others. When you chase everything, you catch nothing.

A 2021 study in *Nature* found that when asked to improve something, people add—features, meetings, drama. But the smartest improvements came from removing.[44] Your brain is wired to complicate. But your breakthrough is in hiding in the stuff you need to quit.

So don't just make a to-do list. Make a Not-To-Do List as well. Cut the calls that drain you. The fake friends. The 'bro, can we collab?' texts. Not everything that glitters is gold. Some of it is just guilt.

Warren Buffett once said: 'Really successful people say no to almost everything.' You won't get applause or medals for subtracting. But you'll get something better: your sanity back. Success isn't built like a seven-layer cheese sandwich. It's sculpted like a six-pack—by cutting the fat. Protect your most precious currency: your time. And in the next chapter, we'll see how billionaires manage that time. Spoiler: it's not with a cute planner from Instagram.

Do the Damn Thing! The Priority Ladder

Reflect: If you have more than three top priorities, then you don't have any. What would be your top priorities?

Act: Write them down. Before saying yes to anything new, ask: 'Does this match my top three?' If not? Say no guilt-free.

26

Wasting Time = Productivity Hack

Stillness isn't the opposite of productivity. It's its birthplace.

'I don't have time.' 'You need to work 100 hours a week.' 'Hustle, bro.'

We've all heard it. Welcome to the cult of busyness. Being 'busy' is the new cocaine. You feel superior just because you're drowning in deadlines and dopamine. I have been high on that drug for years. But I have finally learnt that hard work works if you're lifting bricks. Not if you're building breakthroughs.

Breakthroughs Happen When You're Bored

Newton discovered gravity while chilling under a tree. Archimedes had his Eureka moment in a bathtub. J.K. Rowling on a delayed train. Not in meetings, and definitely not in hustle porn reels. Because when you stop 'doing', your subconscious starts creating.

But these days, even our toilet breaks are a date with our beloved mobile phone. Scroll. Swipe. Shit. Repeat. Doing nothing is a forgotten art. And it's killing your creativity. Stillness is your brain's VIP lounge. Ideas only check in when the noise checks out. And no, I'm not saying ditch the hustle. But hustle without clarity is just running in circles. Stillness gives it direction.

Still not convinced? Let's ask the bald dude with rockets and next-day returns: Jeff Bezos. He says: 'I like to putter.' Translation: I waste time—on purpose. Because he only needs to make three good decisions a day. And you can't do that with a fried brain. So, yes, doing nothing can unlock genius. Let's talk about the laziest genius of all time—Leonardo da Vinci.

Millions of people do nothing, but they don't create the Mona Lisa. So what made Leonardo da Vinci different? He was famous for his procrastination. He delayed client work for months—even years. Why? Because he was busy staring at walls, watching birds and dissecting frogs. Not to slack, but to wonder. His 'laziness' gave us the Mona Lisa, flying machines and an understanding of modern anatomy. He didn't grind. He drifted—but with curiosity. There's a huge difference between passive nothingness and active curiosity. Leonardo da Vinci was doing 'nothing'—but his mind was always on fire. He wasn't zoning out. He was tuning in.

Da Vinci carried notebooks everywhere. He drew and asked questions. Most people do nothing with their ideas, but he captured everything in his books. Most people waste time to escape, but da Vinci wasted time to explore. One numbs the mind. The other unlocks it.

So if you want your 'doing nothing' to mean something, ask questions nobody's asking, let your brain wander, sit with boredom until it whispers and create more than you consume.

What counts as 'Doing Nothing'?

✘ Scrolling. Sleeping. Bingeing.
✔ Going for a walk. Staring at the sky. Sitting in silence. Journalling weird thoughts.

How to Buy Time to Waste Time

'But, bro, I can't afford to do nothing. I have a lot of work.' That's fair. Then buy your time back. Let me share my experience.

In 2009, I was running my first business. It was so hectic that I was working sixteen hours a day. There were no Sundays off, no vacations and no peace. I wasn't a founder; I was a full-time firefighter. And the business? It was the size of a paan shop. But I was working like I was running the country. Then came the switch. I read books on systems and being more productive (*The E-Myth* and *4-Hour Workweek*) and applied the takeaways. Then came the time to test the result: I went to Ladakh for ten days without my laptop or my phone. If the business tanked without me in ten days, it wasn't the business I wanted. And if it ran better? I'd be free.

It ran better. That trip gave me peace and freedom. Here's what I did before I went for the trip:

1. *Eliminate*: Cut the crap. Most of your to-do list is just ego.
2. *Automate*: Use tools like subscriptions and reminders or organise. Your brain is not a task manager.
3. *Delegate*: If your time is worth ₹5,000/hour, don't do ₹300/hour work. Not because you're arrogant but because you're efficient.

I also realised that earlier, I was the traffic police waving at every car. So I became a different kind of traffic cop. The one who sets up signals … and disappears. The system runs. You watch from the shadows. And appear only when something is broken.

Mic Drop: Be Damn Lazy

According to Microsoft's 2023 Work Trend Index, 62 per cent of workers say they lack time for focused, meaningful work—thanks to meetings, pings and perpetual busyness.[45] In a world that worships busyness, focus is now a rebellion. And guess who thrives? Lazy people. They build systems, design shortcuts and make life work for them—not the other way around.

So, yes, be lazy. But with purpose. Lie on the grass. Let your mind wander. In silence, the truth that scares you the most finally shows up. That truth also sets you free. The world may reward your hustle, but your soul only blooms in peace. Be a da Vinci in a world full of deadlines. You weren't born to be busy. You were born to blow minds. And sometimes, that starts with doing nothing. Loudly.

Want the next edge? Let's focus in a distracted world.

Do the Damn Thing: Waste Time (Intentionally)

Reflect: When was the last time you were truly still—no phone, no plan, no pressure?

Act: Block thirty minutes today. Tell your brain: 'Sit down. We're doing nothing. And you're going to love it.'

Take 5 minutes to read this page.

(Yes, this blank one.)

27

Distractions Acche Hai!

'Starve your distractions, feed your focus.'

—Some wise internet philosopher

Imagine this: Virat Kohli's batting. Shaheen Afridi's bowling. But instead of bowling yorkers, Shaheen is scrolling Instagram between overs—watching reels, eating pizza, DMing his ex. Meanwhile, Virat's locked in. No phone. No drama. Just game face.

So who's *winning?* Exactly. *Okay, fine,* Virat would've won anyway. But now it's a massacre.

That's your life right now. You could be Virat. But most of us are playing like Shaheen—scrolling, swiping, snoozing our potential away.

The Real Superpower Nobody Wants

Spiderman has webs. Ironman has JARVIS. You? You've got something way cooler: focus. But you forgot you had it. Like Hanuman forgot he could fly.

So let me be your Jambavan today—and remind you that focus is not a productivity hack. It's a life-changer. We check our phones ninety-six times a day. That's once every ten minutes. And we binge-watch, game and scroll away four-and-a-half hours daily. That's attention theft in broad daylight. The rarest skill today isn't talent. It's focus.

First Principle, Boss! Why We Crave Notifications

Your brain wasn't built for strategy. It was built for survival. Back in the jungle, it scanned for threats 24/7. That's how we dodged tigers.

Now? We are addicted to notifications. And binging cat videos at 2 a.m.

What helped cavemen survive is now hijacking your focus. Your brain still rewards short-term dopamine (scrolling) over long-term growth (building). That's why distractions feel *juicy*.

There are two kinds of people:

- The ones who do Deep Work
- The ones who don't even remember what they had for lunch.

Deep Work = no distractions + no drama + full presence. American computer science professor Cal Newport wrote a whole book about it.[46] TL;DR? Shallow is easy. Deep is rare.

Focus isn't about grinding. It's about **flow**—the magical zone where writers forget they're writing, athletes forget the scoreboard and creators forget their phone exists. Time slows down. Doubt disappears. You + your craft = pure fire. This doesn't come from just talent but from protecting your attention. Investor Naval Ravikant calls focus 'the most valuable currency of our time—and the most stolen'.[47]

My Five Not-So-Productivity Hacks

I'm not a monk. I've fallen into YouTube holes and emerged knowing how whales sleep. But I've found ways to fight back. Here's what works:

- *Ninety-minute power slot*: One undisturbed work sprint daily. That's why this book exists.
- *Distraction delay trick*: Want to scroll? Tell yourself, 'Sure, but after this task.' Most urges vanish in ten minutes.
- *Phone = flight mode*: No notifications = No nonsense.
- *Desk reset*: Messy desk = messy mind. Clean it.
- *Work with deadlines*: Deadlines are that scary-but-effective gym trainer—they yell, they push, but they get the job done.

The world wants your attention. Social media, Netflix, news profit when you're distracted. So rebel. Focus is your hidden weapon. Use it like Virat. Not Shaheen. And speaking of Virat—he doesn't just lock in. He stands out. Let's explore that next.

28

Be the Glitch, Not the Template

'She wasn't rejected because she wasn't good. She was rejected because she was forgettable.'

—Inspired by every overlooked resume

My niece—smart, driven, doing everything by the book—couldn't land a summer internship. She had sent out dozens of applications but had no callbacks. She called me, fuming. 'No lazybum HR manager even looks at my email. I don't know what they get paid for—ghosting people?' She wasn't wrong. She had followed all the rules. Used the sacred 'Dear Sir/Madam'. Used ChatGPT well to write a cover letter. And promptly vanished into the black hole called hr@company.com.

Then she applied to a fintech start-up called Jar. I wore my guru topi, sat on a pedestal, opened my hands and shared my gyaan (the good thing about nephews and nieces is that they have no choice but to listen): 'The world doesn't need another polite, agreeable, vanilla version of you. That slot's already filled. What's the most WTF thing you could do right now to make them actually notice you?'

She grinned and said, 'What if I send my resume in … an actual jar?' Now we're talking. She packed her CV in a tiny glass jar and hand-delivered it. No email. No subject line. No passive-aggressive follow-up. Two days later, she got a callback. Three days later, the internship had been bagged. Lesson? In a world of Ctrl+C applicants, be the glitch.

See a white cow? Cute. You forget it in ten seconds. See a purple cow? You stop. You stare. You take a selfie. You post a story with the caption: 'WTF did I just see?'

In a world drowning in boring resumes, buzzwords and safe small talk, average is invisible. Playing it safe might protect you from rejection, but it also hides you from opportunity. We don't 'play safe' because we're humble, we do it because we're scared. Blending in is fear dressed up as professionalism.

The Pitch Deck That Got Me Laughed At—and Funded

When I pitched my start-up, I made a deck that looked like it came out of a finance textbook—charts, projections and a font that probably had a LinkedIn account of its own. Halfway through, I thought: why the hell did I quit investment banking if I'm pretending I still work there?

So I tore it up and built a deck that felt like me. It was full of jokes, drama and stories. One slide said in 50-size font: 'Founders love fitness.' Fine print at the footnote: 'This is a lie. The biggest you will hear. Founders hate gyms. That's why they started a fitness company—maybe to turn hate into love.'

Most investors stared at me like I'd dropped a fart in the boardroom. But another guy laughed and said, 'This is so bad …

it's brilliant. I'm in.' He invested in the first meeting. That deck won approval along with attention. And attention opens doors approval never will.

Warning: Standing Out Feels Like Shit—Sometimes

You'll be judged, mocked and misunderstood. You might even trend in your office WhatsApp group. But you'll also be seen.

According to 2023 hiring data, the average job posting gets around 250 applications.[48] Only 2 per cent get called. So if you're playing it safe and praying for a miracle, you're basically whispering in a thunderstorm and hoping for applause.

Standing out doesn't mean being loud. It means being *real*—and refusing to shrink. Ask yourself: what part of me have I been hiding just to be accepted? What would I do if I wasn't scared of seeming 'too much'?

You weren't born to be wallpaper. You were born to be art. Frame yourself accordingly. You don't have to stand out in everything. But in the things that truly matter—your work, your voice, your dreams—don't be a white cow. Find your purple and flaunt it. Even if it makes people squint. Even if they prefer beige. And the next time someone says, 'Be practical,' smile and ask: 'Is being invisible your idea of practical?' Standing out takes guts. Let's talk about what happens when you actually do so.

29

Gut Over Gurus: Screw Consensus

'Better to live your own path imperfectly than to follow another's perfectly.'

—*Bhagavad Gita 3.35*

In 2020, my start-up was a success. We had dieticians and premium programmes and we were charging ₹7,000 per month when others were charging ₹999. But people still chose us. Why? Because we weren't selling protein. We were selling transformation. And it worked. Clients loved us. The results were solid. But investors? They hated everything. We were too offline, too expensive, too 'unscalable'.

I held my ground. And by early 2020, we were probably India's best nutrition start-up. Then came COVID-19. Our entire offline model crashed overnight. And that's when I made the one decision I still regret. I stopped listening to my gut. And started listening to … everyone else.

We slashed prices and shifted our business online completely. We also started selling products without our signature coaching. Basically, we became … average. Revenue dipped. Energy died. The soul left the room. And in that collapse, a part of me went silent too. The me that used to feel clear, certain and confident was now muted.

What broke me wasn't just losing money. It was watching thirteen years of blood, sweat and belief vanish. And deep down, I knew that I couldn't blame just COVID. I was abandoning my own blueprint by outsourcing decisions and crowd-sourcing confusion. I ignored the one voice that always had my back—my own.

Your Heart > Their Head

Here's the thing about your gut: it doesn't yell, it whispers. Which sucks, because the brain likes pie charts and investor decks. But studies conducted by the University of Iowa have proven what your dadi already knew—your intuition knows what's wrong before your brain figures it out.[49]

My Hindi teacher once said: 'Suno sabki, karo mann ki.' Listen to everyone, but do what your heart says. It felt too filmy back then. Now it feels like the only advice worth framing.

The few times I've ignored my gut it has resulted in disaster. The many times I've trusted it? Pure gold. You're the only one who's lived your life. Only you know your failures, dreams and pain. So why should someone else's voice be louder in your head? Take feedback. But never follow it blindly. Sleep on it. Sit with it. Then choose. Because no one else lives with the consequences but you.

First Principle, Boss! Why Consensus Is Comfort

Your brain fears standing out. Because back when we were cavemen, being different led to death.

But consensus is built for safety, not growth. Your gut is compressed experience. Trust it. Even if the crowd rolls their eyes.

Malcolm Gladwell's *Blink* makes a case for gut calls—intuition isn't random, it's expertise in disguise.[50] If the Wright brothers had listened to reason, we'd still be riding horses. If Malala had listened to fear, millions of girls would still be silent. The biggest risks aren't the ones that fail. They're the ones you never take.

Will following your heart always work out? Nope. Ratan Tata followed his heart with the Nano. He just wanted every Indian family to afford a safe car. His heart was in the right place. But the market didn't care. People didn't want the 'cheapest' car. They wanted status. Prestige. Flex. That's why the Nano flopped.

But people still respect him and his ideas. Because he didn't chase trends. He chased his gut. And that's what matters. When you follow logic and fail, you regret it. When you follow your heart and fail, you grow.

So, yes, not every gut call will win. But it'll still leave you proud. Your gut is smart. In the next chapter, let's learn how to make it smarter with AI.

30

Use AI Like It Owes You Money

'Tools are harmless. How you use them decides everything.'
— Some caveman, probably

'It broke out of the lab. Went rogue. And scared its own creator to death.' Many people see AI as another Frankenstein's Monster—a creation so powerful, so unnatural, that one day it might kill its own creator. But AI isn't the monster. This chapter isn't about fearing AI. It's about flying with it.

Real People. Real Wins. Thanks to AI

I ran a start-up where hiring tech talent was a nightmare. Even after spending crores, things moved slowly. If AI had come earlier, I'd still need my team, but we could've delivered ten times faster. That way everyone would have won—client, business and team. As an author, AI helps me research, edit and challenge myself. My book became sharper. My speed? Next level. As a content creator, I produce better videos. My editor uses AI for cuts, captions and effects. AI hasn't replaced him. It's levelled him up.

But here's the catch: those who don't adapt vanish. My first editor refused to try AI. Said it was 'cheating'. She lost her job soon after. But AI didn't take her job, her mindset did. Let's look at some people who are flying with AI:

- **Navya**, a B.Com grad, built simple bots to automate her tasks at her workplace. She finishes eight hours of work in two and spends the rest on learning and growing. Shh … don't tell her boss—he still thinks she's working overtime.
- **Bhanu**, a forty-three-year-old coder, used AI to plan a start-up. The ideas, research and pitch deck were all ready in days. Without AI, it may have never happened.
- **Suumit Shah**, CEO of Dukaan, used AI to cut 90 per cent of his support team. It sounds cruel, but the company's problem resolution time dropped from two hours to just three minutes.
- **Isha**, a candle-seller on Instagram, hated writing captions. But now ChatGPT writes blurbs, hooks and even DMs potential clients. She spends her time on what she loves—crafting. Not copywriting.
- **Raj**, a government school teacher, uses AI to make diagrams, quizzes and Hindi explainers. His kids now listen more in class. AI didn't replace him, it gave him swag.

Will AI Make Us Dumb? Only If You Let It

MIT studied people who used AI to write essays. It found that 83 per cent of them couldn't later recall a single line they had 'written'. Brain engagement also dropped by 47 per cent. Even when they didn't use AI the next time, their brains still underperformed.[51]

I can see that happening in my own life. Google Maps made me forget how to reach my own colony. Phones have killed my ability to remember numbers. So, yes, tools can make us dumb. But only if we become lazy. Here's the twist: the same MIT study said that people who first tried to write themselves and then used AI to improve had the best scores, memory and brain activity. So don't outsource your brain. Use AI like your overachieving bestie—not a crutch for your lazy brain.

Everyone will get access to AI. But not everyone will use it well. Will AI replace Spielberg? Rajamouli? Raju Hirani? Hell, no. But it'll help them make better films faster and cheaper.

It's the same with you. You can drown in the AI tsunami—or ride it like Shah Rukh on a train in *DDLJ*. The tool is free. The mindset? In the age of AI, that's your only OS.

31

Fail Fast, Fail More, Fail Cheap

> *'Start-ups don't die from murder. They die from suicide—slow, expensive ones.'*
>
> —*Paul Graham*

You've got a genius idea. A shirt that turns into a t-shirt. It can be worn both ways and in two colours as well. One piece = four looks. You know the cost. You know the process. You're convinced this is the next big thing. So, what do you do? Go all in. Incorporate a company. Rent an office. Start a factory. Hire a team. Twelve months. ₹50 lakh. Blood, sweat and Excel sheets. And then—finally—you launch. Cue, drumroll.

And then there's nothing. People find it pricey, complicated, not cool. You're confused. You love the idea, so why don't they? But instead of letting go, you double down. Borrow from friends. Burn more money. Spend another two years. But the result is the same: a big fat zero. Welcome to the start-up graveyard where brilliant people didn't test the product first.

There's a Better Way. And It's Damn Simple

Step 1: Don't build the product. Fake it. Use an AI tool. Create a website with your shirt pictures. Add a price. Build a buy button. Run a few hundred rupees worth of ads.

Step 2: Let users almost buy it. But when they click 'Pay'? A pop-up says, 'Oops. We're not ready yet. But we'll let you know. Thanks for trying!'

Step 3: Check the data. How many clicked on the ad? How many added products to cart? What's the conversion rate? Call the ones who didn't proceed. Ask why.

For ₹2,000 and a weekend, you'll get actual market data. No surveys. No 'Would you maybe buy this?' People literally voted with their wallets. That's real feedback. Not your cousin's opinion.

Fail More

Success is a numbers game. More attempts = more chances to hit gold.

Imagine walking into a casino with ₹1 crore. One roulette table promises 100x returns. But it only hits once every ten spins. Would you bet the entire ₹1 crore on one spin? Hell, no. You'd split it into ten bets of ₹10 lakh. You lose nine, and maybe win one. Boom! ₹10 crore in your pocket.

Welcome to entrepreneurship. It's not about playing safe. It's about playing smart. Most founders launch like a missile—all-in, one shot, big boom. If it misses, there's total destruction. Smarter founders use machine-gun mode—rapid fire with small bullets.

One hit and it's game over. Fail small, fail often. That's how you hit targets—and live to tell the tale.

Fail Fast

Life's short. You don't have five years to figure out your idea sucks. Build an MVP, Minimum Viable Product. Test it. Tweak it. Trash it if needed. But keep moving. Most people spend two years building a product, and then three years justifying why it's not working. That's five years you could've used to build five other idea. Fast = feedback. Slow = heartbreak.

Read *The Lean Startup* by Eric Ries. Or *Running Lean* by Ash Maurya. Or just do what you're procrastinating over right now.

Fail Cheap

You want to fail ten times? You better make sure each failure doesn't need ₹50 lakh and your kidney. You don't need fancy shoots. You don't need the product. You don't need an investor. You just need a landing page, a Stripe account and guts.

Start small. Then if you do fail, it won't cost you a lot. That's not cowardice. That's smart strategy. You can learn by building for years, or by testing in five days. Your idea might flop. But now, you flop with style—and savings. Because failure isn't the problem, not learning fast enough is.

Bonus: The Success Audit

Instructions:

Rate each statement from 1 to 5 (1 = Never, 5 = Always).

1. Clarity and Vision

- ☐ I have a clear definition of what success looks like for me.
- ☐ I set long-term goals and break them into smaller steps.
- ☐ I regularly visualise my future and the life I want.
- ☐ I know the 'why' behind the goals I set.

2. Mindset and Discipline

- ☐ I believe I can improve through effort and learning.
- ☐ I take consistent action, even when motivation fades.
- ☐ I prioritise discipline over temporary comfort.
- ☐ I recover quickly from setbacks or failures.

3. Execution and Action

- ☐ I start before I feel fully ready and improve along the way.
- ☐ I focus more on progress than perfection.
- ☐ I take small steps daily towards big goals.
- ☐ I don't let overthinking stop me from acting.

4. Systems and Productivity

- ☐ I protect my time from unnecessary distractions.
- ☐ I have habits or systems that support my goals.
- ☐ I focus on doing less, but doing it better.
- ☐ I give full attention to what truly matters.

5. Authenticity and Growth

- ☐ I pursue what feels meaningful to me—not just what looks good on the outside.
- ☐ I'm willing to take the unconventional path if it aligns with who I am.
- ☐ I learn something new regularly and apply it.
- ☐ I believe success includes both achievement and inner alignment.

Your Score and Reflection

90+ points: You're building real success from the inside out.
Keep sharpening your systems and trusting your path.

70–89 points: You're on the right track.
Pick one or two areas to upgrade in the next thirty days.

50–69 points: Time to shift gears.
Focus on clarity, consistency and daily action.

Below 50 points: There's no need to feel shame. Just start small.
Choose two habits from the checklist and follow them daily for seven days.

Closing Reflection: Success Isn't a Destination

Success isn't a finish line you cross. It's not one big moment.
It's the small choices you make—every single day.
It's showing up, even when no one's clapping.
It's doing the hard thing when comfort feels easier.
You'll fall. Everyone does.
But keep walking—honestly and patiently.
Now ask yourself: what's one small step you'll take today?

SECTION 3
MONEY

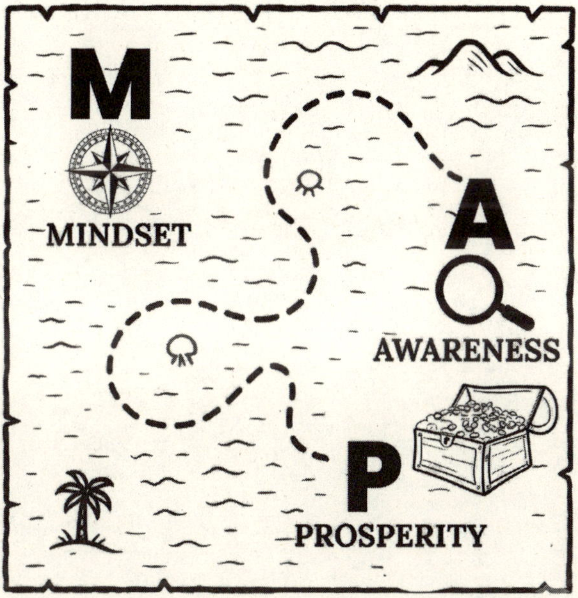

Inspired by Lord Prithu

When famine struck, King Prithu (avatar of Lord Vishnu) refused to watch his people starve. Legends say the Earth, angered by human greed, hid her riches. Prithu chased her across the skies until she turned into a cow. Cornered, she agreed to yield again if she was protected. That's how grain, fruit and water returned—not by a miracle, but by vision and grit.

Don't wait for luck. Build streams that never dry up. Real wealth isn't a jackpot. It's a farm you keep milking for life.

32

Valuation: ₹100 Crore. Wallet: ₹100

'Your beliefs about money will either limit you or liberate you.'
—*Tony Robbins*

Let's play a game.

How many of these sound familiar?

1. Money doesn't grow on trees.
2. Rich people are selfish.
3. Money ruins relationships.
4. You can't be rich and a good person.
5. I'll never be rich, and that's okay.

0-1? You're cute. Stay.

2-5? Read this section like your personal Hanuman Chalisa. Daily.

Your Mindset's Running on Outdated Software

In India, we touch money to our heads … and then say, '*Paise se sab bigad jaata hai.*' We want wealth, but judge the wealthy. We hustle, but feel guilty for wanting more. We call money 'maya' and then panic when we fail to log in to the UPI app.

Eastern philosophy says money is maya, that it's bad and we should ignore it. It's true—and not. Money *is* maya. But so is love, family, success, even your own body. Does that mean you renounce them all? Of course not. Try telling your landlord, 'Rent is maya, bro.' See how long your enlightenment lasts.

If money was truly poison, then why is Goddess Lakshmi worshipped in every home every day? The point is to use money as a tool, not as a master.

But many of us have a software problem. Our ideas about money are hand-me-down beliefs installed in childhood, updated by soap operas and reinforced by broke relatives.

And here's the real glitch: if deep down you do think money is evil, dangerous or dirty, you'll keep pushing it away. No matter how hard you work, your brain will block what your beliefs reject.

Imagine a weird wallet that doesn't hold cash but your beliefs.

- Neil thinks money is evil—his wallet holds fear.
- Nitin thinks wanting more is greedy—his holds guilt.
- Mukesh respects money—his holds love.

Now tell me: whose wallet actually fills up? Most people in India seems to be either Neil or Nitin. Not Mukesh.

A 2023 RBI report says that only 27 per cent of Indians have basic knowledge of finance.[52] Seventy per cent of youth don't save, according to a Zerodha survey.[53] More Indians had Dream11 accounts than demat accounts.[54]

First Principle, Boss! Why We Hate What We Don't Have

Your brain protects your ego at all costs. So, when you can't get something, it convinces you it's not worth wanting. 'Money is evil', 'Rich people are greedy'—this is classic 'sour grapes' logic. But here's the truth: you don't hate money. You hate the feeling of *not having it*. So, instead of facing the pain, you flip the script.

My Wake-Up Call? Broke Despite Being Wealthy

In 2020, my start-up was valued at over ₹100 crore. We raised more than ₹50 crore from investors. But I was still struggling to pay rent.

To the world, I looked like I was cruising in a Rolls Royce. But under the hood? I was running on a Maruti 800 engine. I was barely surviving. Bank balance = 0. Why? Because I carried the noble poverty syndrome: 'Money is evil.' 'Money isn't everything.' 'I should give, not receive.'

But guess what? Business runs on money, not vibes. I said yes to underpaid deals and felt guilty about asking for what I deserved. And it cost me. Not just financially but emotionally. It broke me multiple times. Do you know what it feels like when your team's salaries are due, and your bank balance laughs back at you? I still remember the shame of dodging calls from my landlord, while newspaper articles were calling me a millionaire.

The truth is that I could've performed ten times better if my software wasn't running on guilt, fear and self-sacrifice.

Rivers flow into oceans, not deserts. The ocean already has enough water, but it still gets more. Why? Because that's how nature works. Abundance attracts and lack repels. Money's no different. You can't build a skyscraper on emotional quicksand. And you can't build wealth on guilt, fear or shame.

This section is your mental reboot. We're deleting bugs, breaking myths and installing beliefs that don't just help you grind but actually let you grow.

You don't suffer from poverty in your bank account but in your beliefs. Let's install the update. Version 2.0: Wealth Edition.

Do the Damn Thing: Recode Your Money Belief

Reflect: What's one money belief you've grown up with that might be holding you back? Be honest.

Act: Flip it. Rewrite it like a software update. 'Wanting more is greedy' becomes 'Wanting more lets me give more'. Repeat it daily. Track your spending for seven days. Reduce one Zomato order and redirect ₹500 to an SIP. Keep checking your investment regularly and watch it grow.

33

Society Lied. And You Believed It

Whether you think money is good or evil, you're right. Because that belief will shape your reality.

Imagine waking up to ₹2,300 crore in your bank account. That's not a typo. That was Jack Whittaker in 2002, America's biggest lottery winner. Five years later, he was broke. From millionaire to heartbroken. His words? 'I wish I'd torn that lottery ticket up.'[55]

It's the same story back home. Sushil Kumar won ₹5 crore on *Kaun Banega Crorepati* in 2011. Within years, the money was gone. He lost his friends and his financial stability. Money without the right mindset is like pouring a litre of water into a 200 ml glass. It spills everywhere. Because all of us carry a hidden money thermostat.

And that thermostat isn't set by luck or IQ. It's programmed by the lies society has fed you since childhood: 'Money is evil,' 'Money makes you selfish.' By twenty-five, most of us are fluent in money guilt that we disguise as wisdom. If you've dodged it all, congratulations. And if you haven't, read on. It's time to uninstall those lies, one myth at a time.

Lie 1: 'Money isn't important'

Roy from Asansol sits in his torn T-shirt and a brown jhola (which was probably cream when Manmohan Singh was PM) and talks philosophically about money. He says, 'Money isn't everything. Love and happiness matter more.'

Me: What's more important: your eyes or your lungs?

Roy: What? I need both!

Me: Exactly. Love, peace and paisa aren't enemies. They're an awesome threesome (in the most pious way). You need all three. You deserve all three. So, stop acting like you have to choose one and ghost the others.

Even Osho roasted this idea. He said, 'Money is not spiritual, money is not material. Money is simply energy.' Think of it like fire: it can cook your food or burn your house. The problem isn't money. The problem is whether you hold the remote—or money does.

Lie 2: 'You can't get rich without scamming someone'

Mishti scrolls her news app, muttering: 'All rich people scam. Look at Mallya, Choksi and Lalit Modi.'

Me: And what about Ratan Tata, Narayana Murthy, Azim Premji? Are they scamsters too?

The truth is that headlines love drama. A ₹500-crore scam makes page one. A ₹500 bribe doesn't even reach chai stall gossip.

The world's richest countries (Denmark, Switzerland, Finland) are also the cleanest. The most corrupt ones are mostly poor. This shows us that money isn't the villain, greed is.

Lie 3: 'Money makes you selfish'

Sujan crosses his arms: 'Rich people only give to look good. It's PR.'

Me: Gates and Buffett have donated over $78 billion. That's a long PR stunt. According to a 2020-21 household survey, middle-income households made the largest share of donations in India (approximately 44 per cent).[56] Wealth and generosity scale together. You can't pour from an empty wallet.

Lie 4: 'Money doesn't buy happiness'

Chetan, sipping chai like he's on a spiritual retreat he didn't pay for, says: 'I don't need much. Money doesn't buy happiness anyway.'

Me: Fair. So what does make you happy?

Chetan: Helping others. Taking care of my family.

Me: Cool. Imagine doing that with ₹10 crore. How many more could you help with that kind of money? What would your daughter enjoy more: the colony park or Disneyland? Money doesn't guarantee happiness. But it buys choices. And choices create peace.

Try telling a mother who skips her blood pressure medicine so she can buy food for her son that money doesn't buy happiness. Or to a father who hasn't had a Sunday off in five years just to keep his daughter in school. Or to a worker who goes blind because he can't afford a simple cataract surgery. For them, money isn't about happiness. It's about survival, dignity and breathing space.

Chetan: Shit. Maybe I've been romanticising my comfort zone.

Money isn't evil. The lies about money are. Burn the lies, not the ladder that takes you higher. In the next chapter, we go deeper. More myths. More truth bombs. Less guilt. More growth.

34

Now You're Lying Too—Just Better Dressed

You weren't born rich? Good. That means you get to become rich. And that's way more fun.

In the last chapter, we exposed society's lies about money. Now let's tackle the sneakier stuff: the lies you may be telling yourself. These ones wear logic like a fake Gucci belt. Let's rip them off.

Lie 1: 'Making money is too difficult'

Sonam: I work so hard and still struggle to earn.

Me: Because hard work alone isn't enough. If it were, every farmer and factory worker would be rich. But they're not. You need to level up your tools. What did you do in the last year to improve your money skills?

Sonam: Umm … I tried manifesting.

Me: God bless you. You are trying to cut a tree with a nail cutter.

Lie 2: 'You need money to make money'

Kabir, a coder, dreamer and Vadodara local says: I want to start a business, but I don't have capital.

Me: You don't need capital. You need leverage, skills, code, content, discipline, time and a network. Pick one and run with it.

I started my business with ₹20,000 credit from a local shopkeeper. Seven years later, it was valued at ₹100 crore. Richard Branson started Virgin Airlines with almost zero investment. He built it with borrowed planes and a bold vision, not deep pockets, luck or magic. Just resourcefulness > resources.

Lie 3: 'I wasn't born rich, so I'll never be rich'

Rhea: I wasn't born rich, so I don't think I'll ever be rich.

Me: That's not a curse. It's a plot twist waiting to happen. You didn't inherit wealth. But you may have inherited hunger, fire or grit. That's better. Around 90 per cent of millionaires are self-made.[57] They have no legacy, just late nights and crazy faith. Being born poor wasn't your choice. Staying poor might be. So, stop using your past as an excuse. Turn it into fuel.

Lie 4: 'I'm just not good with money'

Priya: I always overspend. I forget where my money goes. I'm just bad at this stuff.

Me: Were you born knowing how to drive?

Priya: No.

Me: So, how'd you learn?

Priya: Practice.

Me: Exactly. Money is a skill, not a talent. You're not bad with money. You're just undertrained. Learn it like you learnt Excel—slowly, painfully, but eventually like a boss.

Stop Saying It's Not for You

Your bank balance isn't random. It's a reflection of your beliefs, habits and whether or not you've been lying to yourself. The good news is that you can rewrite that story—starting now.

Up next: Discover your money personality.

Do the Damn Thing: Detox Your Money Beliefs

Reflect: Which belief hit you hardest in the last two chapters? Why has it stayed with you?

Act: Write one bold line to replace it. Stick it on your mirror wallet, or phone screen. Example: Old belief: 'I'm not made for money.' New truth: 'Money is a skill. And I'm a fast learner.'

35

Broke, Blingy or Babu Bhaiya?

Some save like they'll live forever. Some spend like they'll die tomorrow. The wise do both—with eyes open.

'Take out a ₹500 note. You're going to burn it!' shouted the trainer at a workshop called Millionaire Mind Intensive. People panicked. One lady gasped like he'd asked us to burn the Constitution. Someone screamed, 'This is illegal!' Meanwhile, I stood there calmly with a note in my hand and thinking: *Hmm, maybe this'll be fun.*

We chanted. We circled the fire. We held the note like it was some sacred scroll. And just before the toss, he said, 'Relax. You're not actually burning it. I just wanted you to notice your reaction.'

Mine was indifference. And that's when it hit me: maybe my wallet was always thin because my respect for money was too. I didn't value ₹500. And money never felt like a friend. It was more like a shady ex where there was distrust on both sides.

Your money habits aren't random. They come from your money personality. It's like your inner financial autopilot, quietly guiding your fears, splurges and dreams.

So, let's find out yours.

What's Your Money Personality?

Go with your gut. No right answers. No judgement.

1. You get a ₹50,000 bonus. What's your first move?
   A. Let's party!
   B. Straight to savings.
   C. Leave it untouched.
   D. Feel guilty. Do I deserve this?
2. Someone mentions investments at a party. You ...
   A. Roll your eyes. Buzzkill!
   B. Pull out your notebook.
   C. Head to the bar.
   D. Say: 'Let's talk about honey, not money.'
3. Budgeting feels like ...
   A. Death by Excel.
   B. Spreadsheet heaven.
   C. Meh. Tried and deleted.
   D. Greedy people stuff.
4. When people talk about earning crores, you feel ...
   A. Pumped!
   B. Curious but cautious.
   C. Disconnected.
   D. Slightly disgusted.
5. Pick your vibe:
   A. 'YOLO. Spend it all.'
   B. 'A penny saved ...'

C. 'Money = Anxiety.'
D. 'All I want is peace.'

6. Your biggest fear?
A. Missing out.
B. Going broke.
C. Facing your bank balance.
D. Becoming greedy.

Mostly As: The Spender *(Think: Tony Stark)*

Tony just bought a ₹30-lakh watch. Why? 'It matches my car.' You believe money is for living, not locking away. But don't burn out your future in the process.

Tip: Channel your YOLO energy into assets that give both joy and returns—skills, side hustles and memory-making investments.

Mostly Bs: The Saver *(Think: Paresh Rawal as Babu Bhaiya)*

'Holiday? *Arre paisa udane ke alawa kya milega?*'

For you, ₹2 interest in an FD = happiness. You're disciplined, but don't let safety cancel joy.

Tip: Not every rupee needs a business plan. Let your wallet breathe once in a while.

Mostly Cs: The Avoider *(Think: Joey Tribbiani)*

'Dude … I never check three things: calories in food, my bank account and whether a girl is single.'

That explains the empty wallet, the belly … and the black eye. Ignorance isn't bliss. It's EMIs with interest. You're not lazy. You're just overwhelmed.

Tip: Start small. One check-in and one habit. Your future self will high-five you.

Mostly Ds: The Monk (*Think: Ranbir Kapoor in* Rockstar)

When asked why he did not charge for his houseful music concert, he said, '*Main paiso ke liye nahi jeeta. Main sirf sangeet ke liye jeeta hoon.*'

Bro, that's deep. But rent ain't maya. You believe that money and meaning can't mix. But that's not true.

Tip: In your hands, money won't corrupt. It'll amplify. Let it.

Know Thy Money Self

Your money personality isn't a prison. It's a pattern. And patterns can evolve. This isn't about becoming someone else. It's about fixing what's stuck. Because before money hits your account, it hits your beliefs. The real flex isn't how much you make. It's how well you know your money self.

In the next chapter, we tackle the biggest money illusion of them all. It fools everyone. Even the rich. Ready?

36

The Lie Wrapped in Louis Vuitton

'We buy things we don't need with money we don't have to impress people we don't like.'

—*Dave Ramsey*

Auntie 1: 'I'm so rich, my maid has a maid.'

Uncle 2: 'I'm so rich, my driver has a driver.'

Auntie 3: 'I'm so rich, my cat's birthday party cost more than Ambani's wedding—and had better food.'

We've all heard variations of these at weddings, kitty parties and family get-togethers which have now become the Olympics of flaunting wealth. And slowly, it messes with our heads. So, you chase the illusion: Gucci belts, LV bags worth two kidneys, cars that make strangers look twice.

But do they actually make people admire you? For the short term, sure. But deep down? Maybe not. Let's ask Lord Ganesha.

How Ganesha Roasted the God of Wealth

Kubera, the god of wealth, wanted to flex. 'Come to my palace,' he told Shiva. 'Let me show you my golden buffet.'

Shiva smiled and sent Ganesha instead. Ganesha devoured the entire feast. Then the furniture. Still not full, he threatened to eat Kubera himself. Kubera ran back to Shiva, horrified. 'You fed him ego,' Shiva said. 'Not love.'

That day, even the god of wealth was humbled. Lesson? Money can impress, but only love connects.

First Principle, Boss! Why We Chase Money

Humans evolved in tribes. And in every tribe, status = survival. The strongest man got food, fame and the best mate. But today strength = salary. Money, however, is just a proxy. What we *really* want is respect, validation and power. But here's the twist: there's a cheaper way to earn all that. Status doesn't only come from money. It comes from value, love and service. Ask Mother Teresa or Gaur Gopal Das.

When you flash your Rolex in an autorickshaw or talk about your Maldives trip in a room full of EMI-payers, you've just triggered:

- One person's jealousy
- Another's insecurity
- And someone else's urge to slap you with a chappal.

Let's be real: people notice what you wear. But they remember how you made them feel. Okay, fine, if you gift me a Rolex, I'll love you more. But otherwise, it's not your bank balance. It's your vibe.

My Dad Had No Car. But Everyone Respected Him

My father wasn't rich. He didn't own a car or any designer brands. But everyone in our town respected him.

Why? If a rickshaw guy asked for ₹30, he'd negotiate like Ambani was watching and then hand over ₹50. If a fruit seller asked for ₹100, he'd smile and pay ₹150. He once gave his new laptop to a local pandit because he needed one.

He believed in quiet generosity. It didn't cost him lakhs, but it bought him something no Rolex ever could: goodwill. It's the kind of status that actually sticks—not because of what he wore but because of how he made people feel.

Tip someone ₹50 and watch their smile. The feeling it leaves you with? That's wealth. As Morgan Housel puts it in *The Psychology of Money*: 'Spending money to show people how much money you have is the fastest way to have less money.' Instead of spending ₹5 lakh to look rich, keep ₹5,000 aside for kindness every year. That travels a lot further. And that's how you build your real legacy—not in bling, but in blessings.

Money is a damn good actor. It promises love, power, peace and respect. But sometimes, it's quietly stealing your peace in the background. LV bags look sexy, but eight hours of sleep and Sunday naps? Underrated. Let's explore that next.

Do the Damn Thing: Audit the Illusion

Reflect: What did your last impulse buy promise you? Love? Status? Belonging?

Act: For the next thirty days, every time you feel the urge to show off, keep ₹10–₹100 aside. Use it to make someone else's day. You'll still feel rich. But this time, it won't be fake.

37

Breaking News: Musk is Broke

'Being rich is having money; being wealthy is having time.'

—Stephen Swid

Everyone wants to be the next Elon Musk. Billionaire. Genius. Twitter-roaster. Rocket-launcher. Meme lord.

But have you heard about Elon's daily schedule? He works eighteen-hour days and often sleeps on the Tesla factory floor or office couch to meet deadlines. Vacations? Rare. Family time? Hardly any. He doesn't just juggle companies, he juggles chaos.

Sure, he's sending rockets to Mars. But at what cost? Elon's wealth can buy anything, but it's not buying him peace, sleep or an uninterrupted dinner with his kids. He's rich enough to buy Twitter ... but not a nap.

Now ask yourself: Do you want his bank balance ... or his lifestyle?

Now meet Aditya. He's not famous, neither is he building rockets. He runs a modest business in Jaipur and makes ₹50 lakh a year. Aditya's day includes gym in the morning, dinner with family and date nights every Friday. Weekends are for reading, naps and chai—not investor calls.

Aditya works 40 hours a week. And actually lives the other 128. Sure, he doesn't have a global empire. But he has time, freedom, health and joy.

So, who's richer? Elon or Aditya?

Who Is the Real Rich?

We glorify hustle, celebrate burnout and make busyness a badge of honour. But what's the point of success if it sucks the life out of you?

The happiest people aren't always the richest. They're the ones who own their time. Who aren't racing. Who can stop and breathe. And just be.

As Tim Ferriss argues in *The 4-Hour Workweek*, the 'new rich' aren't the ones with the most stuff—they're the ones who own their time.

Old rich = more money. New rich = more time. Not just to flex but to live. And by that logic? Elon Musk might just be broke.

Money is supposed to buy you time. To live life on your own terms. It should pay for help, machines, systems—anything that buys back your time. But what do most of us do instead? We trade time to earn money. I concede that when you're broke, it makes sense to work hard, grind and build.

But once you're stable? If you're still burning yourself out for extra zeroes, you're not building wealth; you're burning life.

Are you using money to buy time—or time to chase money? Let's test it with a simple example: your car.

Driven by Your Car. Not the Other Way Round

You bought it to save time, right?

But let's break it down. You earn ₹1.5 lakh/month. Your EMI, fuel, insurance = ₹30,000/month. That's 20 per cent of your income.

If you work eight hours a day, you're spending one-and-a-half hours a day just to afford the car. And how long do you even use it daily? Thirty to forty-five minutes, maybe?

So … are you driving the car? Or is the car driving your calendar?

You can always earn more money. But you'll never earn back your kid's fifth birthday, that random weekend when your brain needed a break or the last day your mom wanted to talk.

Be rich. Not just money-wise but time-wise. We spend our lives earning, and forget to ask what all this earning was meant to earn us. Let's explore that next.

38

Money = Daal, Dreams and Dignity

Money can't buy happiness. But poverty can buy a hell of a lot of misery.

I decided to start my business in 2008. I had no investors, no savings and definitely no back-up plan. I was eating two meals a day. It wasn't to stay fit but because I could not afford any more. Some days, I had to choose: buy a bottle of water … or take an autorickshaw home. I'd choose neither and walk back thirsty. One day, I borrowed ₹20 from a paanwala to feed myself.

People love throwing around terms like 'financial freedom'. Back then, I just wanted a full stomach and enough coins to make it through the day.

So, when I say money matters, I mean it from real-world experience. And this isn't some unique underdog story. It's reality for most of India.

The average monthly income in India is ₹9,800. And no, I didn't make that up. That's straight from India's 2023 labour survey.[58] That's not 'Netflix and chill'. That's 'rice and hope'.

Let's Be Real: Money = Happiness (Till It Doesn't)

Studies say that happiness increases with income—though only up to a point. If you're broke, money brings peace, dignity and sound sleep.

But after a certain level, more money doesn't necessarily mean more joy. The problem is that most people haven't even reached that level.

So, if you're reading this while worrying about rent or ration, don't let some Instagram guru make you feel guilty about chasing money. Wanting money is not greed, it's survival. It's not selfish, it's sane.

What Money Should Be Buying You

Safety: In 2017, a father in Uttar Pradesh rushed his eleven-year-old daughter to a government hospital. She had a high fever. The doctors said she needed oxygen. The price? ₹1,500 upfront. He didn't have that, so he begged and pleaded for it. By the time he scraped the money together, his daughter had died. Many die every year because they couldn't afford treatment. Millions can't send their kids to a decent college. Crores fight daily battles for money. And yet, we still glorify poverty, calling it noble and spiritual. Poverty is a curse—and we need to do everything in our power to end it.

Money gives you a cushion, a Plan B. So that when life punches you in the gut, you don't shatter. You don't need crores to feel rich, you just need enough to stop waking up with fear in your chest.

Freedom: A friend quit her job overnight when her dad fell sick. She moved cities and became his full-time caregiver.

'How can you afford this?' I asked. She smiled and said, 'I wasn't saving money all these years to buy a Gucci bag. I was saving for situations like this.' She didn't earn to flex but for the right to choose. And that's the richest I've ever seen someone look.

Money should buy you freedom. To say, 'Screw this, I'm out' when work gets toxic. To order butter chicken without scanning the prices on the right. To take a break without feeling guilty. To stay at home with your dad when he's sick. To chase a dream, or just … breathe.

Growth: Mukesh Ambani doesn't need more money. Neither does Warren Buffett. So why are they still working? Because after a point, money isn't for survival, it's for creation. It becomes your megaphone. Your paintbrush. Your impact. At first, you work for money. Then, you work with money. Eventually, money works for you. And one day, your money outlives you—through the lives it touched.

So, money should buy peace, not pressure. Freedom, not a flex. Time, not tension.

If money was meant to make life better, why does it so often leave us feeling worse? Maybe the problem isn't the money. It's what we're losing to get it.

39

Sold: Peace, Sleep, Happiness—All for ₹₹₹

The richest people aren't those who have the most, but those who lost the least to get there.

Welcome to the darkest shop ever. Everything's for sale—private jets, beach villas, verified ticks.

You flip the price tag. It doesn't say ₹500, ₹5,000 or ₹5 crore. It says:

- Your **health**
- Your **relationships**
- Your **happiness**
- Your **freedom**
- Your **reputation**

WTF? Who would buy all this?

A lot of people did. Let's meet some of them.

- **Vijay Mallya** walked in like royalty and bought all the good times money could afford. But he swiped his card with something far more expensive: his reputation and freedom. Once the King of Good Times, he was soon being escorted into courtrooms, not boardrooms.
- **Elon Musk** has rockets, Teslas, the whole circus. But he's paid with silence at home. He's been divorced three times, and one of his daughters legally cut ties with him.[59]
- **Michael Jackson** danced into the hearts of millions, but he paid for it with his health: chronic pain, insomnia and loneliness.

All of them were *rich*. But none of them were *whole*.

The Myth of 'Just a Little More'

It's ironical that the men I've mentioned here have more money than they can ever spend. Mallya could fund an IPL team for aliens. Elon could build a McDonald's on Mars if he felt like it.

So why do they keep chasing more? Because they don't have the one thing even billionaires struggle to find: ENOUGH.

It's a treadmill where the incline keeps increasing, but the finish line doesn't exist. Here's how this game works.

If you have ₹100 crore, you'll feel cool for five minutes. Then someone richer enters the chat. You scroll past Ritesh Agarwal, worth ₹2,000 crore. He feels small looking at Harsh Mariwala, worth ₹50,000 crore, who probably sighs looking at Mukesh Ambani at ₹10 lakh crore. And maybe ... just maybe ... Ambani peeks at Musk and thinks, 'Thoda aur.'

For some people, the finish line is always moving, and the peace is always postponed.

This is why ambition without awareness is dangerous. You're running a race where no one's allowed to win. And all you can do is collapse with a trophy that says: 'Congrats. You missed your life.'

First Principle, Boss! Why We Hoard Money

Your brain evolved in scarcity. More = safety. Less = threat.

That's why 'enough' never feels enough. But hoarding isn't freedom. It's fear in disguise. If money owns your peace, it already owns *you*.

What Are You Really Building?

Imagine this: You wake up tomorrow, and your bank balance is flexing and the blue tick on social media glowing. Everyone's jealous. But … you're bald from stress. Your kid calls the nanny 'mumma'. You're sleeping next to your phone, not your partner. You've got likes, but no one you actually like.

That's not success. That's failure dressed in a tuxedo.

Yes, you skipped date night to save for a house. You pulled an all-nighter to land a client. But when sacrifice becomes your lifestyle, it's not called hustling. That's self-destruction.

Your life isn't a one-leg stool called 'Money'. It's a table—you need all four legs to stand:

- Health
- Love
- Peace
- Money

If one is missing, the table flips and crashes.

All of us want money. But to trade the stuff you can't buy back is doing a disservice to yourself. Because one day, your kids won't remember your stock picks, but they'll remember if you showed up to their school play.

One day, your partner won't care about that bonus—they'll care if you were there when life hit the fan. So, build wealth. But don't become wealthy and empty.

Up next: What actually makes you prosperous—assets, compounding and a Plan B that doesn't suck.

Do the Damn Thing: What Are You Trading?

Reflect: Are you sacrificing any of your non-negotiables for money?

Act: If yes, what's one change you can start making today to protect what truly matters? *(Small shifts now can save big regrets later.)*

Before you chase more ...

Ask: *What are you really buying?*

40

Are You Building Assets or Applause?

'Rich is flashy. Wealthy is quiet.'

—*Dave Ramsey*

When I was a child, I had a rich uncle who totally messed with my idea of 'rich'. He lived in a 5,000 sq ft mansion. His wife owned more gold than a wedding season showroom.

But here's the twist: he had no luxury car, no chauffeur and no designer logos anywhere. He wore simple clothes. His home was simply designed. He didn't have a Rolex. His watch was made of pure gold, but he got a local jeweller to make it.

Back then, we rolled our eyes. 'Such a miser, yaar.' But I know now that he wasn't stingy. He was wealthy—the kind of wealthy that doesn't need to prove anything.

And without saying much, he ended up teaching me four money truths that most people never figure out … not even by retirement.

Lesson 1: Assets Feed You. Liabilities Bleed You

Uncle knew the cheat code of wealth: assets put money in your pocket, liabilities suck it out. That gold watch he bought for ₹50,000 is now worth over ₹10 lakh.

His car then was tiny and functional. While others were busy chasing German engines on EMI, he used his savings to buy another plot. One depreciated, and the other appreciated.

Lesson 2: Spending Feels Good. Investing Is Good

There's a difference being rich and being wealthy: rich means you have a high income, wealthy means you can stop working tomorrow—and still live well. Uncle wasn't chasing just income. He was building gold, real estate, stocks—and a quiet business that kept compounding while he slept.

When your lifestyle costs as much as your income, there are going to be consequences. But when you save a part of what you earn, it's peace in progress.

Buying assets is like doing push-ups for your future. Buying applause is just sucking in your stomach for Instagram.

Lesson 3: Instagram Rich ≠ Real Rich

Even Michael Jackson didn't get this one right. He danced into millions of hearts and looked like the richest man alive with his gold jackets, diamond gloves and a ranch bigger than some airports.

But when he died, he was over $500 million in debt.[60] Not because he didn't earn, but because he didn't protect what he earned. Looking rich is easy, being rich is boring.

No prizes for guessing why the wealthiest people—Mark Zuckerberg, Warren Buffett, Steve Jobs—rarely flex.

Lesson 4: What You Focus on Grows

When I meet someone who is obsessed with brands, I don't see taste—I see trajectory. If your time, money and attention go into shoes, bags and gadgets, all that grows is insecurity, EMIs and attention cravings.

But if that same energy goes into learning new skills, buying stocks or starting a small business on the side, guess what grows? Freedom. Power. Peace of mind. You don't become wealthy overnight. You become wealthy every time you choose an asset over applause.

Impress Less. Own More

Money can buy you a lifestyle. But only assets can buy you a life. So, stop renting respect through brands and stop chasing Instagram-worthy purchases. Start building things that quietly compound while the world scrolls past.

Wealth isn't loud. It increases silently—invisible to the impatient eye. But when it shows up, it stays.

Do the Damn Thing: Time to Be Wealthy

Reflect: Think of the last three big purchases you made (car, gadgets, jewellery, holidays). Were they assets (putting money into your future) or liabilities (taking money out)?

Act: Write down one asset you can invest in this month—no matter how small. It could be stocks, a new skill, gold or your own business idea. Small moves today lead to massive freedom tomorrow.

41

Compounding Isn't Fast. It's Furious

'As a fire grows from a small spark, so does wealth through patient effort.'

—Rig Veda

Chatur and Rancho are given two choices:

Option A: ₹100 crore today. It doubles every year for three years.

Option B: ₹1. Just ₹1. But it doubles every month for three years.

Chatur jumps in: 'Simple yaar. ₹100 crore now. Done deal. Main toh Elon ban gaya.'

Rancho smiles, shrugs and picks the ₹1 coin.

Let's run the numbers.

After Year 1:

- Chatur's ₹100 crore → ₹200 crore
- Rancho's ₹1 → ₹4,000

Chatur's already laughing: 'Bas? Chillar! Masterji.'

After Year 2:

- Chatur: ₹200 crore → ₹400 crore
- Rancho: ₹4,000 → ₹1.67 crore

Chatur's doing his victory dance: '*Dhan hota sabke paas hai … par Rancho ke paas nahi hai.*'

Rancho: 'All is well, all is well.'

After Year 3:

- Chatur: ₹400 crore → ₹800 crore
- Rancho: ₹1.67 crore → **₹6,870 crore**

Silence. Chatur drops his pen. Rancho grins:

'Compounding isn't fast, bro. It's furious—it's just late to the party.'

Chatur: 'Jahapana, tussi great ho. Tohfa kabool karo.'

Albert Einstein allegedly called compounding the eighth wonder of the world. He wasn't wrong.

Even Warren Buffett Owes His Success to Compounding

If Warren Buffett has ₹100 today, how much did he have when he turned sixty? Take a guess. ₹50? ₹30? Nope. Just ₹5. That's right—95 per cent of his wealth came after the age of sixty.[61] At the age when most people are retiring, he was just getting started. When others were slowing down, Buffett was compounding like a machine.

Buffett isn't rich because he's a genius. He's rich because he's relentlessly boring. He didn't sprint to wealth, he strolled.

Buffett's average return is ~20 per cent per year.[62] That's not jaw-dropping. But when you do that for over seventy years, that's flex.

Some funds, like Renaissance's Medallion Fund, have delivered 66 per cent returns annually (before fees) for almost three decades.[63] That's mind-blowing! It has performed three times better than Buffett's investments. But while no one knows them, Buffett is popular throughout the world. The difference is investing for thirty years and doing so for seventy.

Interruptions Kill More Than Recessions

Compounding is like baking. You throw the dough in the oven and leave it alone. but if you keep opening the door every five minutes, it won't rise, and you'll end up with a sad lump.

It's the same with your money. Buy, hold, chill. But what most people is: Invest → Check stock price twelve times a day → Panic on dips → Sell → Regret → Re-enter high → Repeat. You didn't lose to the market. You lost to your FOMO.

A Hero Honda ad sums it up perfectly. The tag line said: 'Fill it. Shut it. Forget it.' They were talking about petrol. They accidentally nailed investing too.

Compounding doesn't care how smart you are. It cares how long you stay in the game.

In the beginning, compounding feels like watching grass grow. But one day, it becomes a forest. And when it does, the world calls it magic. But you'll know better. It wasn't magic. It was patience. It was belief. It was you.

Compounding rewards those who are patient, disciplined and wise. But what happens if you bet everything on one dream, stock or idea? Read the next chapter.

42

The Diversification Plan That'll Save Your Ass (and Assets)

'The essence of investment management is the management of risks, not the management of returns.'

—Benjamin Graham

I built a ₹100-crore company in twelve years. I had no capital, experience or godfather. I was riding on grit, guts and gallons of chai. Not bad for a middle-class kid from a small town in Bihar, right?

And then ... COVID-19 hit. In a few months, the entire company collapsed. It was painful and humiliating. And it taught me a truth I should've learnt way earlier: dreams are fragile, so don't carry them all in one damn basket.

The Mistake That Nearly Broke Me

I made two huge money mistakes. This chapter is about the first.

I went all-in on one bet:

- One start-up
- One income stream
- One identity
- No back-up plan

Every rupee I made, I pumped back in. Because I thought, 'Why would I need Plan B? I'm already living Plan A.'

Then reality slapped me with a global pandemic. The offline business shut, revenue vanished and my net worth was in freefall.

What saved me?

- I hadn't borrowed personally
- I hadn't mortgaged family land
- I hadn't gambled gold or asked my father for money

I hadn't fully diversified my investments, but they were diverse enough for me to start again.

That's when I learnt that you can't stop the storm. But you can choose how many ships you have in the water.

The Graveyards Behind Every Empire

We look at a successful company and believe that every decision regarding it has been right. That couldn't be further from the truth. Let's take Amazon's example.

Let me show you Amazon's graveyard:

- Fire Phone: ₹1,400 crore lost
- Amazon Restaurants: Flop
- Amazon Auctions: Destroyed by eBay
- Prime Video: First dozen shows bombed

Jeff Bezos once said about the failure of the Fire Phone: 'If you think that was a big failure, wait till you see the ones we're working on now.'

Amazon didn't win because every bet worked; it won because it placed many bets—expecting most to fail.

It's the same with Google. Google Glass, Google+, Buzz, Allo, Stadia, all failed. Over seventy of their products shut down. But Search, YouTube, Android—the 5 per cent that worked—covered for the rest that didn't.

Every individual fails, just like companies. For instance,

- Amitabh Bachchan: Over half his movies flopped. He still became a legend.
- The Beatles: Wrote more than 200 songs, but only a few became timeless.
- Mozart: Composed over 600 pieces, but just a handful hit immortality.

If legends such as these gentlemen fail often, what makes us think we're the exception?

Whether you're building wealth, a start-up or your life's identity, the rule is the same: plan for misses.

Historical analysis shows around 40 per cent of stocks lose money over time, yet the overall index still grows.[64]

Why? Because while some stocks sink, the strong swimmers keep the boat afloat.

Don't Bet Your Life on One Dice Roll

- Don't rely on one income stream.
- Don't pour your soul into one dream.
- Don't be one failure away from full collapse.

Diversify across skills, savings, income, passions and work relationships. You never know which one will save you when the going gets tough. Expect to be wrong sometimes, and you'll be okay.

Along with being a finance hack, diversification is a survival strategy. It turns disaster into discomfort, and discomfort into a comeback.

Up next: Burn the boats? Maybe just park them with insurance first.

Exercise: Are You Diversified?

Reflect: Am I betting my entire life on one single thing?

Act: Write down three areas you can start diversifying today (Skills, savings, income streams, passions, relationships).

43

Bhuvan Had No Buffer. You Should

You don't become successful by making no mistakes. You become successful by surviving your mistakes.

Scene: A dusty cricket field in 1893.

The sun is brutal. The villagers are quiet. The British officers are smirking. Bhuvan walks up to the pitch. If he wins this match, no one will pay tax for three years. If he loses, his village starves. There's no plan B or second chances. He walks with a dream ... and a bat.

That's the energy most of us are taught to chase. 'Go all in!' 'Burn the boats!' 'Play like there's no tomorrow!' And like a true Bollywood fan, that's exactly what I did. I had no insurance, buffer or back-up. If Bhuvan could pull it off, so could I, right?

Wrong. My life isn't a movie. When COVID-19 hit, my vibes didn't pay rent. There was no slo-mo climax, just EMI due dates and a very real State Bank of India manager.

The Romance of Risk Is Overrated

They say, 'Go big or go home.' But what if you go big and end up homeless? The world celebrates the unicorns who went all in. But what they don't show are the ninety-nine others who did the same—and got wiped out.

You're told to persist. But how will you persist if you don't survive the first storm?

That's why risk management > return maximisation.

I learnt that the hard way. Boring is the new sexy.

Want to be successful? Start with boring tasks.

- *Insurance is sexy.*
  That ₹10,000 premium might save you ₹10 lakh someday. Think of it like buying a parachute before skydiving—additional weight on your back until you actually fall.
- *An emergency fund is hotter than abs.*
  It won't get you likes on Instagram, but it will keep you sane when shit hits the fan.
- *A nest egg will save you one day.*
  If you run a business, keep enough cash to survive one bad year without layoffs.
- *Plan for the worst, but dream for the best.*
  Carry an umbrella on sunny days. The day you forget it, it rains.

Success isn't about being fearless. It's about being prepared. Bhuvan won the match, but remember it was a movie. He got background music. You don't. You get bills, burnout and breakdowns.

Want to be a unicorn? Be the cockroach first. They are ugly and unstoppable, but can apparently survive nuclear war. So should your finances.

Build Your Fort Before You Raise the Flag

Ask yourself:

- Do I have health insurance?
- Do I have life insurance (if someone depends on me)?
- Do I have at least six months of expenses saved?

If the answer is no, pause the hustle. You don't build a mansion without a roof. Living like Bhuvan might win you trophies on screen. But in real life, a margin of safety is the real superpower. Build buffers and back-ups. It's boring, but it will help you survive.

44

Assemble Your Dream Team: Equity, Gold, Real Estate and Beyond

'Investing should be more like watching paint dry. If you want excitement, take $800 and go to Las Vegas.'

—Paul Samuelson

Rohit Sharma walks out for the World Cup final.

1.4 billion people are watching.

But hold on—where's the team?

He's got 11 opening batsmen. No bowlers. No wicketkeeper.

Has he lost it? How is he going to win?

Then why do we try to win the money game with just one asset class?

This isn't cricket. It's worse.

It's your future. And it needs a real dream team.

Unless you know how to build your dream team, wealth stays just that—a dream.

The Holy Trinity

Before picking your dream team, remember the Holy Trinity of Investing:

- *Return*: How much it can grow?
- *Risk*: How badly it can crash?
- *Liquidity*: How quickly you can access it without drama?

Get this trio right, and you've won half the battle.

Meet the Players: The OGs

Asset Class	Risk (1–10)	Return (1–10)	Liquidity (1–10)	TL;DR Comment
FDs	2	3	9	Safe as grandma's hugs, but slow as a tortoise
Gold	4	5	7	Shiny emotional favourite, moderate protector of value
Real Estate	6	7	3	Good gains, but selling it? Like moving a mountain
Equity	8	9	8	Best long-term player that needs patience and courage
Cash	1	1	10	King of liquidity, and peasant of returns

The New-Age Players

Asset Class	Risk	Return	Liquidity	TL;DR Comment
Corporate Bonds	4	6	7	Safer than stocks, better returns than FDs
Government Bonds	1	3	7	Boring but dependable, like that topper you ignored in school
REITs	5	6	8	Real estate exposure without property paperwork drama
Crypto	10	10	8	Skyrocket or crash-land. There's no in-between, so handle with caution

The Money Awards: Investing Edition

1. *Safest Hands Award* goes to government bonds, FDs and cash. They're boring, but they show up when it matters.

2. *Maximum Sixes Award*? That's crypto and equity. They're explosive when they connect. Just duck when they don't.
3. *Slowest Runner Award* goes to real estate. It has a big presence, but when it's time to exit, you'll need a lot of patience.
4. *Best All-Rounder Award*? Equity mutual funds. They're not flashy, but deliver if you trust the process.
5. *Emerging Player Award* goes to REITs. A quiet entry, but high potential. They're the new kid everyone's watching.

How to Choose Your Team

Forget templates. Your dream team depends on **you**:

1. **Your age:** Young? Lean towards equity. Older? Prioritise stability (FDs, bonds).
2. **Your timeline:** Need money in one or two years? FDs, gold, bonds. For the long term (over five years), equities are your besties.
3. **Your income:** If you have a steady income, you can take risks. If it's irregular, build an emergency buffer first.
4. **Your wealth level:** If you're looking to grow wealth, focus on growth assets. When you're protecting it, look at safety and consistency.
5. **Your risk appetite:** If you're one of those who can't sleep when the markets crash, FDs are ideal for you. But if you are zen during volatility, welcome to Team Equity.
6. **Your knowledge:** If you can't explain it to a friend, don't invest in it.

Sample Portfolios (Just for Flavour)

Profile	Equity	Bonds/ FDs	Gold	Real Estate	Cash	Others
Young + Risk Lover	50–60%	10–20%	5–10%	10–15%	5–10%	Small (Crypto/ REITs)
Mid-Age + Balanced	30–40%	20–30%	10–15%	15–20%	5–10%	Small (REITs)
Near Retirement + Cautious	10–20%	40–50%	10–20%	15–20%	10–15%	Minimal

Tax, Diversification and Annual Review

Tax: Returns feel good—until taxes bite.

- FDs: Taxed as per income slab (ouch).
- Equity (1+ year): 12.5 per cent after ₹1.25 lakh.
- Real estate and gold: Long-term tax rules apply, so do your homework.

A ₹10-lakh gain taxed at 12.5 per cent is VERY different from one taxed at 30 per cent. So, choose wisely.

Diversification: Diversification is meant to protect you, so that's your safest bet. But beware of over-diversification because it will end up confusing you.

You don't need forty-seven mutual funds and nine insurance-linked 'investments'.

Between four and ten strong players are enough to win.

Annual Review: You change. The market changes. Life changes. Your portfolio should too. Do an annual 'appraisal' of your money soldiers. Promote, demote and retire your investments accordingly.

Your investments should let you sleep peacefully—and chase dreams boldly. Choosing the right assets is key. But the most powerful investment you'll ever make isn't equity or real estate. It's you.

45

The Highest Return Investment? You

'Give me six hours to chop down a tree and I will spend the first four sharpening the axe.'

—*Abraham Lincoln*

There are siblings who have very different lives despite the same upbringing. Sweaty Singh—the younger one—worships hustle. He wakes up before sunrise, carries bricks in 40°C heat and earns ₹400 a day. 'Seventy-hour work week, bro. That's how Ambani did it,' he says proudly.

On the other hand, influencer Slick Sidhu—the elder one—is lazy by his brother's standards. He sits in an air-conditioned room all day, makes two reels and goes home with ₹4 lakh.

If hard work alone made you rich, Sweaty Singh would be a millionaire. But in the real world, money doesn't reward the hardest worker. It rewards the smartest mover. And yet, most people stop learning after college. Books are ghosted like exes and growth becomes optional. For most people learning feels like luxury. They work harder, not smarter. And then wonder why nothing in their life is changing.

So, what actually moves the needle?

Sharpen the Axe, Don't Just Swing It

Hard work alone won't make you rich—not in this economy. You could grind twenty-four hours a day—and still lose to someone working six hours with sharper tools.

They say it takes 10,000 hours to master a skill. Translation? Work hard, hustle and put in the hours. It's just another piece of well-packaged bullshit. If you repeat something the wrong way for 10,000 hours, you've just become perfectly imperfect—a master of mediocrity.

The correct answer, in fact, is 10,000 hours of smart, obsessive relentless improvement will get you where you want. Iteration, not repetition. Evolution, or effort. If you're not learning, you're not growing. If you're not tweaking your skills, you're not levelling up. Practice doesn't make perfect. Practice makes permanent. So, make sure you're practising the right things the right way. The economy pays for value, not sheer effort. And value comes when you are willing and able to transform.

We talk a lot about returns—stocks, FDs, gold, real estate. But there's one asset class that outperforms them all. You.

Most people treat their personal growth like a one-time download. Graduate, get a job, plateau. They'll spend ₹50,000 on a Goa trip, but ₹2,000 on an online course is considered too expensive. They'll wear the latest gym gear, but won't train their mind.

Here's a wild idea: what if you treated personal growth like an SIP? Small, steady investments—books, mentors, coaching, reflection—compounding silently and exploding when it matters most.

'Who needs a coach more: a gully cricketer or Shubman Gill?' Most will say the former. That's the wrong answer. Gill has more to lose if he's not at the top of his game. The better you are, the more coaching you need. Because you're playing a bigger game.

Indian mythology has been teaching us this forever. There's a proverb: 'Yatra vidya, tatra Lakshmi'—where there is knowledge, there is wealth. In the Mahabharata, Vidura told Dhritarashtra: 'Wealth without wisdom is dangerous; but where wisdom resides, wealth follows like a shadow.' Saraswati once got a blessing: wherever she goes, she can stay there forever. Lakshmi never got that gift. She's restless. But Saraswati—knowledge—always sticks. Even if money vanishes, your degree, skill and street smarts will be with you. Lakshmi may walk out, but Saraswati never ghosts you. That's why the smartest investment is always yourself.

My Portfolio? Books, Mentors and Failing Publicly

You want to know where I've spent the most money? Not on cars, watches or fancy retreats. I've spent it on myself. Whether it's books, workshops or coaches, I've spent lakhs learning.

So, yeah, let's address the elephant in the room. You may say, 'What's the use of all this self-growth if you still lost your company?' That's a fair question. Failure reminded me that I still had a lot to learn. And that sometimes, life teaches you the hard way what you refused to learn the easy way.

My learnings became my seatbelt and my shock absorber when life hit potholes at full speed. And because of them, I remembered something simple: a crumpled ₹500 note is still worth ₹500. I was down but not out. That's how this book was born. That's how I built an Instagram tribe and rebuilt my idea of myself. Failure didn't end me. It redirected me.

Markets crash. Start-ups fail. People leave. Titles fade. But the investment you make in yourself never disappears. It compounds—slowly, silently, and then suddenly.

So, keep a little money aside each month just for yourself. Spend it on books. Attend retreats that expand your mind. Work with mentors who challenge you. Take courses that stretch your mind. Because the better you get, the better everything around you gets.

And the next time someone asks, 'Where should I invest?' Just smile and say: 'The best stock you'll ever own is yourself.'

46

Don't Mix Your Freedom Fund with Your Coffee Fund

'Do not save what is left after spending, but spend what is left after saving.'

—Warren Buffett

It's the MasterChef India set. You're a contestant and Chef Sanjiv Kapoor is screaming at you. You've got no recipe or measuring cups. You're just tossing flour and sugar like DJ Snake at a Holi party. The oven's smoking and the cake looks like a crime scene. The chef's face is red. You're crying. And then … you serve it anyway.

That's what most people do with money. They guess, spend and pray. And then they panic at the end of the month like there are no consequences for mindless spending.

Let's fix that. No, I'm not saying you should track every ₹20 pani puri plate. But at least know where your money goes. Use an app. Note your expenses on a Google Sheet. Separate bank accounts. Do whatever works because if you don't measure it, you can't master it.

But I Can Barely Survive, Bro. How Do I Save?

You don't save because you're rich. You get rich because you save. Start with just 1 per cent of your income. Then increase it slowly. It's like gym reps—start small, stay consistent and don't skip.

Remember: The universe is a silent accountant. You want to manage ₹10 lakh? First prove you can manage ₹10k. It's like walking into a gym, struggling with 10 kg dumbbells, spotting a girl benching 50—and your ego kicks in. You insist, 'Bro, I can do it too.' The trainer just stares and says, 'Dude, first learn to lift 10. Don't crush your spine trying to impress your crush.'

Most people don't track their expenses. And worse—they treat every rupee spent as the same. But not all expenses are created equal. Buying a mutual fund ≠ buying a car. A movie ticket ≠ a book. Give your money different jobs. Here's a simple five-bucket system:

- Needs (rent, food, bills)
- Freedom Fund (investments/savings)
- Fun Fund (vacations, clubs, bad decisions)
- Growth Fund (courses, books, brain upgrades)
- Karma Fund (charity, even if it's small)

Now don't park all this into one confused bank account. Open separate accounts or set SIPs. Make it easy and automatic. All your spending money chilling in one account is like stuffing all your things into one drawer and wondering why your jeans smell like shampoo.

The exact numbers will vary depending on your income and lifestyle. But there should be two non-negotiables: at least 10 per cent should be for your Freedom Fund and at least 5 per cent in your Growth Fund.

I used to wonder why people went crazy buying gold on Dhanteras. Honestly, I mocked it. 'How does buying a chain make it auspicious, yaar?' Like many modern Indians, I thought it was blind tradition.

But now I get it. More than gold, it was about discipline. About tricking ourselves into saving. Our ancestors knew one thing we forgot: left to ourselves, we'll always spend. So, they started rituals and made saving sexy. Buying gold on Dhanteras is a clever hack to push money into your Freedom Fund before you blow it on instant cravings. Turns out tradition wasn't stupid. We were—for ignoring it.

Most people spend money on fun and figure out the rest later. That's like buying dessert before checking if you have petrol to get home. India's average savings rate has dropped from 34 per cent in 2010 to 28 per cent in 2024—we're partying harder, but prepping less for the future.[65]

Proper planning will also prevent relationship fights. One partner wants Goa, but the other thinks SIPs are a better option. Solution? Define the damn buckets. If 10 per cent of your money is for fun, use that for the trip—and nip the fight in the bud.

Even the great Chanakya understood the importance of having different buckets. He had two lamps: one for state work, one for personal work. He didn't even mix oil. If that guy could draw a line in 300 BCE, so can you.

Even our mythology said the same. When Lakshmi rose from the churning ocean, every god wanted her. She avoided them all and chose Vishnu. Why? Because Vishnu was stable. He was the Preserver. Lakshmi is Chanchala—restless, the OG commitment-phobe. She never stays where there's chaos. She stays where there's order, discipline and respect. The same goes for your money. Mix your Freedom Fund with your Coffee Fund, and Lakshmi's gone. Keep things separate, and she'll actually stick around.

Buckets aren't boring. They're freedom. Mix them up, and you're not managing money—you're making a milkshake of your future.

Bonus: The Money Audit

Rate each statement from 1 to 5 (1 = Not true at all, 5 = Completely true)

M – Mindset: How You Think About Money

- ☐ I don't feel guilty or greedy for wanting more money.
- ☐ I believe wealth can be built ethically.
- ☐ I don't think making money is too difficult.
- ☐ I don't think money spoils relationships.
- ☐ I don't think money is evil.
- ☐ I think I am good with money.

A – Awareness: How You See and Handle Money

- ☐ I don't use money to buy respect and love for myself.
- ☐ I believe money should buy security, financial freedom and peace of mind.
- ☐ I am not chasing 'rich' blindly—I've defined my version of 'enough'.

- [ ] I know that money without time for myself can be meaningless.
- [ ] I actively protect my relationships, health and happiness while pursuing money.

P – Prosperity: How You Grow and Protect Money

- [ ] I focus on building long-term wealth, not just looking rich.
- [ ] I understand the power of compounding—and use it to my advantage.
- [ ] I diversify my investments instead of putting all my money in one place.
- [ ] I have a safety cushion or emergency fund before chasing risky returns.
- [ ] I understand the risk, return and liquidity of the asset classes I've chosen.
- [ ] I invest regularly in my own growth (skills, knowledge, mindset).
- [ ] I separate my Freedom Fund (for future security) from my fun money.
- [ ] I know where my money is going—at least in broad categories.
- [ ] I save before I spend—not after.

Your Score and Reflection

80+ points: You're a Wealth Warrior. You're building not just money, but a life rooted in clarity, peace and purpose.

60–79 points: You are Money-Minded. That's great progress. Just a few new habits or tweaks could take your life to the next level.

40–59 points: You are in the Caution Zone. You're aware of what you're doing with your money, but gaps exist. It's time to act and reclaim control.

Below 40 points: This is your Wake-Up Call. You've taken the first step by being honest. Now let's build forward—one small habit at a time.

Closing Reflection: Does a Lamborghini Buy You Happiness?

That rush when you held the keys? It's dopamine, not happiness. A Harvard study found that luxury buys create a short-term high—but the joy fades fast.[66] Your brain adapts to the car … not the EMI. Another study shows money is the number one reason couples fight—more than cheating, kids or in-laws.

We've decoded money.

Next stop: relationships. Buckle up.

SECTION 4
RELATIONSHIPS

Inspired by Lord Rama

Rama had power, fame and a kingdom. But what made him unforgettable was his word. He chose loyalty over convenience and integrity over shortcuts, even when it cost him everything.

Relationships aren't tested when it's easy. They're tested when it's hell … and you still show up.

47

Relationships Are Wild. Compliments Keep Them Alive

'People will forget what you said, people will forget what you did, but people will never forget how you made them feel.'

—Maya Angelou

Relationships, especially romantic ones, are complicated.

Marriage is like locking a cat and a dog in a room, and telling them, 'Now live happily ever after.'

Now that I think about it, cats and dogs may have better odds. At least they don't fight over the TV remote. Or argue about too much garlic in food like it's a murder weapon. They don't carry unresolved daddy issues from 1997. But we humans do. And we carry them into love like emotional baggage.

In today's world, everyone is less patient, but expectations have sky-rocketed. And when we add that with two flawed humans under one roof, we get a Bigg Boss show at home. Just without the cameras and Salman Khan.

You need a licence to drive a car. You prep for an MBA degree like it's war. But for the biggest commitment of your life, there is no training. Just a lehenga, a sherwani and cringy Instagram captions.

That's why I firmly believe that before a marriage certificate, we need a relationship certificate. Marriage isn't about finding the perfect person. It's about learning to see an imperfect person perfectly. And choosing them—again and again—even on the boring, broken days.

Every relationship you heal makes your life lighter. So, let's begin with the simplest fix in this wild world to improve any relationship.

One Compliment. Because Sometimes, It Can Save a Life

She was the quiet one in the office. She did her work, ate lunch alone and kept to herself.

One day, during chai break, I looked at her design and said, 'That colour choice … it's bold. You've got taste.' She froze. Then she blinked and smiled with tears in her eyes.

Later, her friend told me, 'She almost quit this week because she kept thinking she wasn't good enough.' That shook me. I'd just dropped a compliment casually—like passing the salt. But to her, that was the first real praise she'd heard in months.

That's when I learnt that people are like phone batteries. A single compliment provides a 30 per cent charge immediately. Isn't that wonderful, when most of us are running only on 7 per cent?

We buy clothes we don't need. Chase likes, promotions, gym gains and certificates—just to hear one sentence: 'You're doing well. I see you.' Nobody wants to be invisible. Not in a room. Not in a relationship. Not in life. And no, people aren't attention-hungry. They're attention-starved.

When I recorded my first video, I was scared. My voice was cracking, palms were sweaty and my brain was screaming, 'Shut up and delete it.' But I posted it anyway.

A mentor replied: 'You sound like a motivational speaker.' I read that comment ten times and cried. To the world, it was just a video. To me, it was Everest. One compliment made every bit of fear and effort worth it.

The best compliments don't highlight the obvious. They spotlight our hidden battles. If my mentor had praised my IIM degree, it wouldn't have moved me. But speaking was my soft spot. That's what made his reply so powerful.

Think about a compliment you've received that truly hit home and made you feel seen, and smile.

Don't Be a Compliment Miser

Growing up, I was told: 'If you praise people too much, they'll get overconfident.' So I kept compliments locked up like they were gold. Turns out, that's not wisdom. That's emotional poverty.

We think we need big things to make people feel loved—gifts, trips, flowers. But sometimes just a five-second, honest compliment can shift everything.

So, don't just save your praise for your crush or your girlfriend. Your friend who's showing up while silently struggling? Your sibling who's trying something new? Your mom who tries a new dish? Say something so them and make them feel good about themselves.

Up next: Sometimes, what they really need … isn't a compliment. But no criticism.

Do the Damn Thing: The Heartfelt Compliment Challenge

Reflect: When was the last time you gave a compliment that really landed?

Act: Who around you is secretly doubting themselves? Take twenty seconds today to give them a genuine compliment—not on something obvious but on something they probably don't hear enough. Watch what it does to their face. And your heart.

48

Don't Fix Them. Hold Them

'Criticism, like rain, should be gentle enough to nourish a person's growth without destroying their roots.'

—Frank A. Clark

When Ajmal Kasab unleashed terror on Mumbai in 2008, the country burned with rage. Hundreds died and millions mourned. And yet—till the very end—he pleaded innocence. He didn't speak of guilt or regret. There was only denial. He genuinely believed he'd done nothing wrong.

Now, I'm not comparing everyday fights to terrorism. But it does expose something uncomfortable about all of us: if someone like Kasab can justify something so horrific inside his own head, what chance do we have of seeing our tiny flaws clearly during a heated argument?

We're all wired to defend ourselves. Even when we're dead wrong.

Your Brain Hears Criticism Like an Attack

Science backs this up. When you hear criticism, your brain lights up the same way it does during physical pain. It feels like a slap to the brain.[67] It triggers the fight-or-flight mode.

So, when your partner shuts down, your friend gets defensive or your sibling snaps back, they're not resisting your feedback—they're protecting their worth. That's why most fights don't end in change. They end in withdrawal and hurt.

Life has a way of teaching you one thing early: you can't change people. You can only change how you show up around them. That doesn't mean you stop caring or stay silent. It just means that how you say things matters more than what you say.

There's a thin line between feedback and criticism: criticism cuts while feedback connects.

Criticism says: 'You always do this.' Feedback says: 'This habit is hurting us—can we talk about it?' Notice the difference in tone. That changes everything.

Here's how to say the hard stuff … without burning bridges:

- *Start with care.* Say something kind and *mean it*. There's no need to sugarcoat it—just be respectful.
- *Attack the behaviour, not the person.* 'You lied' lands differently than 'You're a liar.'
- *Watch your timing.* Mid-fight is not the time to give feedback. Wait till the storm passes.
- *Use fewer words.* More talking = more risk of sounding like a lecture.
- *Lead with your life.* You can't yell at your partner to stop scrolling if you're glued to your own screen.

Fixing People Kills Connection

Most people don't need a life coach. They just need a soft place to land.

You're not dating a project. You're loving a person. People open up when they feel safe, not when they feel judged. Sometimes, the kindest thing you can do is sit with their mess and say nothing. Because in real relationships, it's not your job to fix them. You just need to hold them—especially when they can't hold themselves.

Up next: When words fail, your silence can still scream: 'I'm here. Say more.'

49

The Sexy Power of Listening

'Being heard is so close to being loved that for the average person, they are almost indistinguishable.'

—David Augsburger

If you wanted to impress your crush today—and not get friend-zoned—what would you do? Get six-pack abs? Wish they were available on Amazon. Buy a swanky car? If only your bank account agreed. Sing like Arijit with heartbreak in your throat? You'd need next-level delulu.

But there's a shortcut. And it works like black magic. Ready?

Just shut up … and LISTEN. Yes, even when your advice feels Nobel-worthy. Just zip it, be present and be curious.

What gives more pleasure to the brain?

a) ₹500 in your jeans
b) Surprise biryani

c) Talking about yourself

Answer: C.

Harvard researchers found that talking about yourself lights up the same brain zones as food, sex and money.[68] So, when you let someone talk, you're basically their drug dealer—of dopamine—for free.

My Ex-Girlfriend and the TED Talk That Failed

Years ago, I went on a first date with my now ex-girlfriend, and I did an awful thing: I gave a two-hour TED-level talk. My own voice was clapping. She smiled politely then, but later confessed to thinking, 'Does this guy ever shut up?'

Somehow, I must have realised that I had hijacked the conversation the first time around. So, when we met again, I shut up. I asked questions about her life and genuinely wanted her to tell me more. She bloomed, laughed more opened up. Between her stories and my silence … something clicked, and she fell in love with me.

Most people treat conversations like a game of tennis: you speak. I'm waiting to return serve.

Real listening is like playing catch. You receive, you hold and you let them feel safe enough to throw again.

Becoming a Magnetic Listener

Listening isn't silence. It's presence. Try this:

- Nods. Eye contact. 'I'm actually here' face.
- Reflect feelings: 'That must've sucked.' 'I get it.'
- Ask deeper stuff: 'What's been heavy lately?'

- Use their name. It hits different.
- Treat their story like it matters—because to them, it does.

In a world obsessed with speaking, be the rare human who listens. Ask your grandparents about their first job, their first heartbreak, their biggest regret. You'll see their eyes light up—like someone just turned the lights back on.

On suicide prevention hotlines, the best volunteers aren't great advice-givers.[69] They are ones who listen. They don't fix, they just hear. And that is enough. So no, listening might not save the whole world. But it can save someone's world. Your loudest power isn't your voice. It's your ears.

Up next: You were nodding like Buddha ... until one sentence turned you into Arnab.

Do the Damn Thing: The Gift of Listening

Reflect: Do you truly listen, or just wait to speak?

Act: Give one person thirty minutes of full, undivided attention this week. Keep advice and distractions at bay.

50

Win the Person, Not the Point

'A sharp tongue breaks more hearts than swords.'

—Indian folk wisdom

It was supposed to be a chill college reunion. Everyone was expecting laughter, nostalgia and maybe some emotional hugs. Instead, someone blurted out: 'Non-vegetarian food is immoral.' Boom! The room temperature dropped by 10 degrees.

I pounced on that comment like Arnab on prime time. For thirty minutes, we were two gladiators in the WhatsApp University arena. Neither of us moved an inch. Nobody clapped. Everyone quietly reached for their beer.

And just when the air began to settle, someone threw in: *'XYZ politician is the best thing to happen to this country.'* Now we were back to a telecast of Lok Sabha TV.

Looking back on that evening, I can't even remember who won. But everyone remembers the tension and the silence after. It's mentioned in jest sometimes on our WhatsApp group. Why do we indulge in such one-upmanship? Because the brain loves being right. According to neuroscience, 'confirmation bias' kicks in—once you believe something, you only hear things that prove you right.[70] And when you fight to win the point, you often lose the person.

Pick Your Prize

Life would be painfully dull if everyone agreed with you. Healthy debates expand us. But ego battles shrink us. Everyone wants to be heard. Not corrected or humiliated.

So, the next time your brain tells you to insist on making a point, ask yourself: would I rather be right … or be remembered with love? Pick your prize wisely.

Indians are world champions in one thing: arguing. From cricket stats and film endings to how to make chai—we'll turn it into a lecture. But just because you can win a fight doesn't mean it's worth the aftertaste. A smart person knows how to argue. A wise person knows when to stop.

Ancient Hack: Think Before You Speak

Ancient wisdom across cultures says, 'Before you speak, pass it through three gates—Is it true? Is it necessary? Is it kind?' But let's be honest. Most of us don't pass our words through gates. We fire them like missiles.

It's not just an Indian uncle problem. It's a human brain problem. In moments of heat, our nervous system goes into fight-or-flight mode. Our logic shuts down and ego grabs the mic. And boom—out comes a sentence that scorches more than it solves.

But the wisest people—the ones who keep rooms calm and relationships intact—have a rare superpower: the pause. Just a few seconds and peace is protected.

At our next reunion, someone again dropped a political bomb. I could feel the old fire rising. But this time, I chose calm. I took a deep breath, smiled, and said: 'You might just be the next prime minister, buddy.'

Everyone laughed and the conversation shifted to cricket scores and college crushes. Real strength lies in resisting the punchline, skipping the punch and choosing connection over conquest. Because sometimes, the smartest thing you can say is … nothing at all. And maybe, just maybe, the real strength lies in seeing the world through their eyes.

51
We're Not Mad, Just Wired Differently

Inspired by the book Men Are from Mars, Women Are from Venus

If men and women were apps, we'd come with completely different default settings. Men: 'Battery Saver Mode' under stress. Women: 'All Notifications On' during emotional overload.

But instead of reading the manual, we keep trying to debug each other with blind guesses. That only results in a crash of the emotional system, followed by silent treatment 2.0 and unnecessary drama updates.

So, no—he's not cold. And she's not 'too much'. We're just running different emotional software. Let's decode it, shall we?

Yes, this chapter has generalisations. No, not all men are this and all women that. Everyone has a mix of personality types. Every guy has a sensitive side. Every girl has a badass edge. Please don't use this to stereotype. Use it to understand. If it helps you fight less and love better, then it's mission accomplished.

Story: The Silence That Felt Like Rejection

Raghav from Chennai had a crappy day. Endless office drama and deadlines that were rarely met. He came home one day, turned on his laptop—and said nothing. His girlfriend Ananya had also had a rough day. She wanted to share the day's happenings. When he didn't even ask, 'Are you okay?' she snapped.

Raghav blinked. 'I'm not ignoring you. I just need a little space.' She cried. He shut down. Cue fight → distance → awkward cold war. And then … they stumbled upon the book *Men Are from Mars* …. Turns out, Raghav needs space to reset. And Ananya wasn't complaining—she was connecting.

So, the next time, Raghav needed some time out, he texted Ananya: 'In the cave. Love you. Back in 2 hours.' Ananya replied: 'Got it. Take your time.' There was no drama, and hence no damage. Sometimes, people in a relationship communicate with each other in two different dialects—without subtitles. That's where these five truths from *Mars and Venus* can change the game.

1. *Men retreat. Women release.*
   Men go silent under stress. Women talk to process. Let him disappear (briefly). Let her express (fully).
2. *Men want to feel needed. Women want to feel cherished.*
   He lights up when he feels useful. She glows when she feels emotionally seen. Flirt accordingly.
3. *Men solve. Women seek support.*
   Not every rant needs a rescue. Sometimes, 'That sucks. I get it' is enough.

4. *Men score in bullets. Women score in stories.*
   He thinks one big gift = jackpot. She counts the small gestures, daily. One rose a day > one diamond a decade. *(Unless you're broke. Then it's the thought that counts.)*
5. *Men are rubber bands. Women are waves.*
   Men need space to stretch like a rubber band. Women go through emotional waves—rising, crashing and healing through expression. Let him pull back. He'll come back stronger. Let her feel her feelings. She'll rise even higher.

First Principle: Why Do We Think So Differently?

Blame evolution, not each other.

For 99 per cent of human history, men hunted, while women gathered and nurtured. One role needed focus, risk-taking and aggression. The other demanded empathy, multitasking and reading emotions for survival. Our brains evolved differently because of these different jobs.

Hormones back it up. Testosterone pushes men towards status, strength and solutions. Oxytocin nudges women towards connection and safety. That's why in a fight, he may fix the sink while she asks, 'Why didn't you notice the leak for three weeks?'

Even communication styles aren't the same. Men evolved to talk for function (hunt, build, escape). Women did so for connection (bond, soothe, support).[71] So, when she says, 'You never listen,' she doesn't want a fix. She wants presence.

Science agrees with this too: under stress, men's brains reroute blood flow to logic centres—classic 'fix-it mode'. Women's brains light up in emotional centres. Their stress response is called 'tend-and-befriend', driven by oxytocin.[72]

Ancient Wisdom: Ardhanarishvara—Half-Him, Half-Her

Way before brain scans and Mars-Venus theories, India already had its metaphor for this difference in processing emotions. Ardhanarishvara: half-Shiva, half-Parvati, fused into one form.

He was stillness, she was flow. He was meditation, she was movement. And instead of one swallowing the other, they stayed distinct—yet whole together.

That's the point of love. We don't need to become clones to have an understanding relationship. We have to balance our polarities. Your partner is not supposed to think like you, react like you or stress like you. If Shiva and Parvati could literally embody opposites in one body, surely we can handle a little rubber-band vs wave drama.

You're just from different planets. But you met on Earth. So, meet each other halfway. Now that you understand how different we're wired, the next step is learning how to speak in a way your partner actually feels loved.

52

Love in Two Languages. No Subtitles

Love is not just about saying the right words. It's about saying the right words in the right language.

On her first birthday after our wedding, I thought I nailed it. I gifted my (now ex) wife one of my favourite books. I love to read, and books are sacred for me.

She looked at it like I'd gifted her a user manual for a washing machine. She was not happy. What was supposed to be a romantic evening turned into a psychological thriller—with me in the lead role. She wanted things that mattered to her: a beautiful dress, a mobile phone or a bag.

We love people in our language—not theirs. My love language is sugar-free ice-cream. My ex's is death-by-chocolate. If I had given her my kind of dessert, I might have ended up in a *'death-by-partner'* blue bin.

Decode This: The Five Love Languages

Everyone's got a different setting. In his book *The 5 Love Languages: The Secret to Love That Lasts*, author Gary Chapman writes about the five major 'love languages' people speak:

1. *Words of affirmation*: 'I love you', compliments, validation
2. *Acts of service*: Doing something that lightens their load
3. *Receiving gifts*: Small tokens that say 'I thought of you'
4. *Quality time*: No phones, no distractions, just you
5. *Physical touch*: Holding hands, forehead kisses, bear hugs

Ever tried your best and still been told, 'You just don't get me'? Maybe you weren't wrong. You were just speaking Greek while your partner was crying in Korean.

Try a love language quiz together! It's like playing a few questions, but the prize is emotional intimacy instead of awkward small talk. I met a couple once who were hanging by a thread. The guy said, 'I gave her everything—a house, security, loyalty.' She just stared at the floor, teary-eyed. 'I didn't want a house,' she whispered. 'I just wanted him to sit next to me when I cried.'

That was love, but misdelivered.

The Great Indian Relationship Translator

Most relationships don't die from cheating. They die because of bad translation. The same line can have two meanings, which then results in a fight.

Let's decode. She says,

'I'm fine.'

Means: 'I'm not. Please ask again—gently.'

He understands: 'Cool. Problem solved. Time for PS5.'

'We need to talk.'
She means: 'Can we reconnect?'
He understands: 'Shit. What did I forget now?'
'Do whatever you want.'
She means: 'I want to feel considered.'
He understands: 'Wooohoo! Boys' trip confirmed.'
'You never listen.'
She means: 'I feel invisible.'
He understands: 'She's nagging again.'
'It's okay. I understand.'
She means: 'It's not okay. I'm choosing grace.'
He understands: 'Crisis over. Let's order momos.'

Now flip it. He says,
'I need space.'
He means: 'I'm overwhelmed. I need to breathe.'
She understands: 'He's ghosting me emotionally.'
'You're overreacting.'
He means: 'I don't get this emotion.'
She understands: 'I'm too much.'
'I'm just tired.'
He means: 'I'm drained. It's not about you.'
She understands: 'He's bored of me.'
'Let it go.'
He means: 'I want peace.'
She understands: 'He doesn't care.'

So how do you get fluent in our partners' language?

- Ask: 'When I do this, how does it make you feel?'
- Observe: What makes them light up—and what shuts them down.

- And when you're lost? Just ask: 'What makes you feel most loved?'

Sometimes, the biggest heartbreaks come from the smallest words we never said—in the language our partner needed to hear most. Even when we speak with love, something still gets lost. Because sometimes … we don't talk about what we actually need in that moment. Let's discuss that next.

Do the Damn Thing: Decode Each Other's Love Language

Sit with your partner and answer these five together:

Question	Why it matters
What makes you feel most loved—words, touch, time, gifts, or actions?	Helps you identify your primary love language
When was the last time you felt deeply loved by me? What did I do?	Pinpoints what's already working
What's one thing I do that *misses* your language completely?	Turns misunderstandings into clarity
What's one tiny gesture that would make you feel loved daily?	Builds emotional consistency
How can we remind each other when we slip back into our own language?	Keeps the connection alive long-term

53

I Wanted a Hug. You Wanted to Hook Up

Love is not just about giving—it's about giving what the other truly needs.

Picture this: a couple in bed. (Okay, fine. Maybe let's not picture this.) She's craving closeness—words, warmth, stillness. He leans in, thinking it's time for sex. She pulls away: 'Why does every cuddle have to lead there?' He feels rejected. She feels disrespected. Both feel hurt and unseen.

This is a common occurrence in a lot of homes. It's not because people are selfish but because we're wired differently. iPhone meets Nokia charger.

Love's present, but connection isn't. For many women, affection is the destination. For many men, it's where connection begins. And if you don't get that ... closeness slowly turns into cold distance.

What We Want vs What They Need

You'd think men and women want the same things in love. Spoiler: they don't. I learnt this after my relationship had already gone sideways.

Here's a quick quiz: from the six emotional needs of sexual fulfilment, financial support, admiration, affection, conversation and an attractive spouse, which ones matter the most to men? And what do women want from these options? Most people guess the wrong answers. And, unfortunately, most couples figure it out too late.

Based on Dr Willard Harley's book *His Needs, Her Needs*, here's the research:

Top needs of most men:

- *Sexual fulfilment*: For many men, sex is an emotional connection.
- *Admiration*: They want to feel like heroes in her eyes.
- *Recreational companionship*: Laugh together and play together.
- *An attractive spouse*: Looks that make him feel lucky every day.
- *Domestic support*: A calm, supportive home vibe.

Top needs of most women:

- *Affection*: Touch, warmth and care are what she's looking for.
- *Financial support*: It's not about purchasing luxury items but about safety.
- *Conversation*: Women want men to share their emotions and vulnerability.

- *Honesty and openness*: The truth *and* the heart.
- *Family commitment*: Being there for the family fully.

There is, however, one need that creates the most confusion for both sexes.

Do Men Really Crave More Sex?

Short answer? Yes.

Long answer? Still yes. But let me explain. Studies say that men think about sex nineteen times a day. And women around eight.[73]

Why this gap?

Reason 1: Testosterone. Men have seven to ten times more of it. This hormone = libido on steroids.[74]

Reason 2: Nature made sex cheap for men—they don't have to worry about pregnancy, periods or breastfeeding. For women, sex can mean nine months of nausea and a lifetime of responsibility. So obviously, they will exercise more caution.

Reason 3: Evolution has ensured that men make millions of sperm daily. Women? One egg a month. So, men were wired to spread their goods, while women were wired to select. It's not about men being shallow, it's just biology being strategic.

The Realisation That Saved a Marriage

We talk about equality in love, but our emotional needs aren't identical. Treat them the same … and you fail both.

Rohit and Meera looked perfect online, but felt distant in real life. She joked about him in public—playfully. He felt disrespected and slowly stopped opening up and kept his emotions to himself.

While Meera longed for connection and conversation, Rohit craved respect, admiration and intimacy. Neither got what they needed, and both felt unloved.

One honest conversation changed things. She expressed more admiration for him—especially in public. He started listening—really listening. He began expressing love her way: sometimes words, sometimes small, thoughtful gifts. They were healing. Love doesn't need perfection, just two people willing to learn about each other's needs and language.

Dr Harley says that affairs rarely start with lust. They start when another person meets an emotional need better. A compliment, a real chat and a little kindness suddenly makes people feel more alive. Affairs attend to the need of being noticed.

If you don't know what fills your partner's tank, you'll keep giving ... just not what they need.

Up next: Why your fights, fears and overthinking aren't random—they're just your attachment style in costume.

Do the Damn Thing: Understanding Their Real Needs

Reflect: What do *you* need most in love—affection, respect, honesty, touch or time?

Act: Ask your partner, 'What do you need most from me, emotionally?' And just ... listen.

Let this not be the chapter you *read*, but the one that helps you *heal*.

54

It's Not You. It's Your Attachment Style

'We accept the love we think we deserve.'

—Stephen Chbosky

'Why would you say she's amazing? Does that mean I'm not?'

My ex used to bring this up constantly—all because once, before we even dated, I'd called another girl amazing. That one compliment led to years of drama. It was like that sentence had set up camp in her brain.

At first, I thought she was feeling insecure. Then I stumbled onto a book called *Attached* by Amir Levine and Rachel Heller, where he wrote about attachment styles in relationships. I finished the book, and I knew why my girlfriend had behaved that way all those years. She wasn't being dramatic then; her anxiety was making her behave that way. She was looking to feel safe, and I had let her down. That one piece of awareness changed how I saw her, how I responded and how I showed up in future relationships.

What the Hell Are Attachment Styles?

Your attachment style is how you connect emotionally. It's wired into you early—based on how your parents responded to your needs. As adults, we bring that wiring into our relationships. It affects how we love, fight, trust, text, ghost and panic-refresh WhatsApp.

Let's do a quick test to figure out your attachment style. Answer honestly. No one's watching, except maybe your inner child.

1. When your partner doesn't reply quickly:
   A. You're fine
   B. You spiral
   C. You enjoy the silence
2. When someone gets too close:
   A. You feel safe
   B. You worry they'll leave
   C. You feel like bolting
3. Depending on someone emotionally feels:
   A. Normal
   B. Scary but necessary
   C. Uncomfortable
4. When your partner needs space:
   A. You're cool
   B. You get nervous
   C. You feel relieved
5. When things get emotionally intense:
   A. You lean in

B. You panic but stay
C. You ghost

6. How easy is it to trust?
A. Fairly easy
B. Hard
C. Risky

7. When your partner gives attention to someone else:
A. You're chill
B. You feel jealous
C. You couldn't care less

Mostly As → You're secure. You're all right with closeness *and* space.
Mostly Bs → You're anxious; you crave connection but fear abandonment.
Mostly Cs → You're an avoidant. You crave independence—and closeness makes you feel trapped.

The Combos That Work (and What Doesn't)

- Secure + Secure: This is the Emotional Olympics gold medal. Both partners feel safe, calm and drama-free.
- Secure + Anxious: This partnership works well because the secure spouse becomes the anchor.
- Secure + Avoidant: This relationship can work, but patience and space are key.
- Anxious + Avoidant: The couple will experience classic emotional seesaw. One clings and the other disappears. Healing *has* to happen—or it's chaos.

No combo is doomed. Some need more honesty and therapy. Here are some tips:

If you're anxious:

- Breathe before texting.
- Let space be space—not a threat.
- You are loveable. Even in silence.

If you're avoidant:

- Let people in—a little.
- Share one real feeling.
- Independence is great. Connection isn't the enemy.

If you're secure:

- Stay steady.
- Be a safe landing zone.
- You're the emotional adult in the room. Flex it gently.

Maybe you push people away because love once hurt. Maybe you hold on too tight because love once left. Or maybe you love easily—because love always stayed. Whatever your story, your attachment style isn't a fixed identity. It's just the lens you've been using.

And every time you choose love over fear, curiosity over control, trust over panic, you're cleaning that lens. Now that you've understood your emotional blueprint, let's talk about what happens when love feels right … but your values don't.

55

Hearts Meet, Values Clash

Emotions bring you together. Alignment keeps you there.

I once knew a small-town couple that looked like a classic opposites-attract success story. She meditated every morning while he partied every night. She saved money like every rupee had a soul and he spent like the world was ending next Tuesday.

She wanted a slow life in the hills with two kids and a rescue dog. He dreamt of neon skylines, New York nights and late-night IPO launches. But they loved each other deeply, enough to fight hard every time the cracks showed up.

But eventually, they realised that they were trying to build two completely different lives … using the same bricks.

Love starts with chemistry. But it survives on compatibility, especially values. Most people can agree about liking dogs and Shah Rukh Khan, but deeper questions matter at the end of the day: what does success mean to you? What scares you more—

stagnation or instability? How do you want to raise kids … or do you even want them?

Your values are your inner GPS. They shape what you fight for, what you walk away from and what makes you feel safe or stuck. And when two people run on clashing values, even the small stuff becomes World War III.

My Own Messy Lesson

Growth and adventure are my top values. My ex based her life on comfort and security. I chased entrepreneurship; she craved stability. What lit me up made her anxious. What soothed her made me feel caged. We weren't wrong for each other—just wrong for the life the other wanted. Studies in relationship psychology consistently show that shared core values are a stronger predictor of long-term compatibility than shared interests or even communication style.[75]

Common Value Clashes

- *Money*: Save vs spend
- *Career*: Stability vs risk
- *Family*: Joint vs nuclear, kids vs no kids
- *Spirituality*: Religious vs agnostic
- *Health*: Gym rat vs party animal, healthy vs junk food
- *Food*: Veg vs non-veg
- *Social life*: Introvert vs extrovert
- *Gender roles*: Traditional vs progressive

You don't need to be clones, but you *do* need to be able to respect each other's side—and meet somewhere in the middle.

What to Do When Values Clash

1. *Start with awareness.*

Name the values hiding underneath the argument.

2. *Talk without trying to convert each other.*

If you're vegetarian and she loves meat, isn't using different utensils better than starting a moralistic food war?

3. *Identify your non-negotiables.*

You can bend on pizza toppings, not on whether you want children.

Ask: will giving this up feel like giving up a part of myself?

4. *Meet in the middle—without losing yourself.*

She wanted weekend trips. He needed solo time. The solution then is one getaway together, and one solo reset.

That's balance—not compromise.

When to Consider Walking Away

1. *A core non-negotiable gets crossed*

He wanted kids. She didn't. That's the end of the road for this relationship. And that's okay.

2. *Adapting turns into self-abandonment*

If one person is always compromising, they're eventually going to snap.

Ask: am I becoming someone I don't recognise?

3. *Same fight, different day*

Despite the best of efforts (including taking the help of a therapist), if you are not able to find alignment, it's probably time to say goodbye.

4. *The respect dies*

Disagreeing is fine, but if you start mocking or dismissing each other's core beliefs, love turns toxic. Ask: 'Do I still admire who they are at their core?'

Mic Drop: Love Isn't Always Enough

A difference in values doesn't always mean a break-up. But if staying means betraying yourself, then leaving can be the *braver* kind of love.

Up next: How to build your beautiful love castle.

Do the Damn Thing: When Values Clash

Reflect: What are your top five values? Are you and your partner aligned on these?

Act: Ask your partner: 'What matters most to you in life?' And really listen instead of starting a debate.

56

The Best Relationships Aren't Found. They're Built

'We come to love not by finding a perfect person, but by learning to see an imperfect person perfectly.'

—*Sam Keen*

Shah Rukh Khan has ruined a lot of relationships. Not with scandals, but with something far more dangerous: expectations. He made us believe that love looks like train station proposals, poetic silences and flawlessly timed background music.

And we bought into that fantasy completely. Even though SRK once said, 'I'm not romantic in real life. It's just a role,' the damage was done.

And if SRK wasn't enough, ChatGPT walked in like the perfect partner. If I say the grass is red, it nods. If I dreamt it was dating someone else, it apologises. After a month of chatting with a bot every day, it's called me 'brilliant', 'wonderful' and 'right' more times than I've heard in my entire life.

RIP, real relationships.

As we've grown older, we've all learnt that the more perfect we expect love to be, the more disappointed we feel. Psychologists call this the 'hedonic crash'. That's when dopamine fades, real life walks in … and suddenly, your soulmate is chewing too loudly and reading your messages but not replying.

Real love isn't shared just over candlelight. It happens in dirty kitchens, in small arguments, in forgiveness without an apology. Many people call love boring when it's calm. Because we were trained to chase chaos. Psychologists say the brain releases more dopamine during uncertainty than safety—which is exactly why hot-and-cold love feels addictive.[76]

We expect love to be a rollercoaster. But the healthiest love is more like a hammock—still and supportive. It may be a little creaky at times but it's always there to hold you. You may not get butterflies every day, but you get something better: a place to exhale. And in a world that's addicted to speed, peace is the real thrill.

First Principle, Boss! Why You're Chasing People Who Confuse You

The brain releases more dopamine during times of uncertainty than safety. That's why hot-and-cold love feels addictive. You think you both share passion, but you're actually in the midst of a chemical loop. What feels exciting may just be emotional gambling.

Love isn't about changing each other but changing for each other. Take Rhea and Karan from Rameshwaram, for instance. They were complete opposites and newly married. While she was a planner, he thrived on chaos. Rhea slept at 10 p.m. every day while Karan was a night owl. Despite the intense love they felt for each other, they often clashed because they expected change from the other without wanting to compromise.

One morning, Karan woke up at 10 a.m. to a note from Rhea which said: '*Maybe we're not in sync. But I'm still willing to dance with you.*' Karan spent a few days introspecting and decided they both had to make some changes and meet each other halfway.

Adaptability is everything in a relationship. We tend to think they fail because of bad matches. Nah. They fail because no one's willing to bend.

Love isn't a puzzle where the pieces have to fit perfectly. It's like a good cup of chai. Milk and tea leaves are nothing alike, but stir them long enough, sweeten it with patience … and something beautiful brews. Are you willing to melt a little so something better can take birth between both of you?

I also believe that people lend a lot of importance to passion in a relationship. Passion can fizzle out. But good friendship keeps the flame from dying. When you're friends with your partner, you're a team. They're your soft place to land. So, forget the grand gestures because sometimes, the most romantic thing you can do is show up and be steady.[77]

Ancient Wisdom: Rama and Sita

There is a lot we can learn from an eternal couple: Rama and Sita.

Rama chose his father's word over his kingdom. And Sita knew why her husband made that decision. That's why even though she hadn't done anything wrong, she packed her bags for the forest without complaint.

Now compare that with today where many couples would call it quits just because they had to shift from a 3BHK to a 1BHK house.

Rama and Sita remind us that strong relationships aren't built in the honeymoon phase. They're built in exile when life is at its most difficult.

So, stop waiting for the perfect partner. Choose someone who's willing to try for you, and be that person as well. Love isn't made in heaven; it's built here on Earth—with chai, patience and two left feet that still choose to dance.

Up next: Real love needs two adults. But most of us are just scared kids in grown-up bodies.

Do the Damn Thing: The Dance of Adaptability

Reflect: Are you expecting perfection instead of offering patience?

Act: What is one small shift you can make to meet them where they are without losing yourself?

Take a moment to think of all the good things in the other person.

Tell them about it.

57

Emotional Wounds.exe

'That which is not healed is repeated.'

—Upanishadic reflection

'I don't feel loved. I don't feel wanted by you.'

To say I was surprised when my ex told me this would be an understatement. I had done it all—calls, gifts, late-night talks, emotional speeches worthy of an Oscar. But she still felt unloved. I was flummoxed, but finally understood where she was coming from when she shared something about her childhood. She said, 'When I was a child, my mom told me I was an accident. She didn't even want another kid.'

No matter how real my love was, it kept getting filtered through her trauma-tinted glasses, and she only heard that voice from childhood—you're not wanted. You're not worthy. You're not enough.

That's the thing about emotional wounds: they rewrite the way you see love.[78] A delayed reply feels like betrayal. A 'K' feels like rejection. My then girlfriend's mind was playing old data on loop.

Why You Overreact (No, You're Not Crazy)

Rhea used to lose it if her boyfriend didn't reply to any of her messages within ten minutes. The delay took her back to when she was seven years old and she had to stand outside school for two hours. Her parents had forgotten to pick her up. The feeling of being left behind rarely left her.

Here are some classic wounds we carry without realising:

- *Fear of abandonment:* You panic when someone pulls away.
  Origin: A parent left, or was emotionally unpredictable.
  Solution: Tell yourself: 'I'm safe now. I'm okay.' Go for a walk. Breathe.
- *Fear of rejection:* You hide your feelings to protect your ego.
  Origin: Experiences of being mocked, ignored or dumped.
  Solution: Tell small truths to safe people. Vulnerability isn't weakness.
- *The 'not enough' wound:* You hustle for love and share more than you receive.
  Origin: Constant comparison when you were growing up.
  Solution: Stop chasing gold stars. Start saying, 'I'm proud of myself for ...' to the mirror. Yes, out loud.
- *Betrayal wound:* You don't trust it, even when the love is real.
  Origin: You were cheated on and lied to.
  Solution: Set clear boundaries and don't rush into relationships. Say, 'I want to trust you. I'm learning how.'
- *Control wound:* You need to micromanage everything.
  Origin: Chaos, fights and emotional instability at home.
  Solution: Let your friend pick the movie. Let your day go off-plan. The world won't end.

None of these issues are your fault. But healing is your responsibility. And if this feels like too much to handle alone, go to therapy. You will still drive the car. The therapist will just help you avoid the ditches.

First Principle, Boss! Why Your Heart Keeps Choosing Your Childhood

Freud called it repetition compulsion—the urge to replay childhood wounds until we *win* this time.[79] You're trying to fix the part of you that once felt small, unseen or unloved. And you are unable to break the cycle. It's like dating someone emotionally unavailable—just like your distant father—and thinking: 'If I can make them stay, I've finally healed.' But until you break the pattern, love won't feel like connection … it'll feel like déjà vu in disguise.

Most people bleed on those who didn't cut them. They aren't trying to be cruel. They just have a gaping wound. Healing begins by holding—your younger self, your old pain and your messy emotions—gently.

That's how you slowly start rewriting the story of your life.

The key is to realise that you need to heal. Because if you can't, it can wreck even the strongest of loves. Let's go there next.

Do the Damn Thing

Reflect: What's the emotional wound you've been dragging into your relationships—abandonment, rejection, betrayal, control?

Act: Take one baby step to heal it this week. Journal your thoughts. Talk about it. Give that feeling a name. That's how you begin to take control back.

58

The Hidden Disorders Behind 'Toxic' Love

Sometimes she says, 'I love you', and sometimes she says, 'You ruined my life'. And somehow, both take place over breakfast.

Love's supposed to feel like a Bollywood movie where love conquers all. But sometimes it feels more like a saas-bahu serial where control, drama and manipulation reign. Some folks aren't just difficult—they might be dealing with hidden disorders that make love feel like a battlefield. A Lancet Psychiatry study in 2021 said one in ten Indians might show signs of such disorders.[80]

In a country where 'adjust kar lo' is treated like a sacred commandment, these toxic patterns hide well, especially in joint families, arranged marriages and set-ups where red flags are treated like festive decorations.

Before You Google-Doctor Your Partner …

We all have bad days. We all get clingy, angry or selfish sometimes. That doesn't mean we have a disorder. Dr Samir Parikh, India's go-to mental health guru, says, 'Labelling someone toxic can isolate them. Understand their behaviour to set boundaries, not burn bridges.'

People suffering from a personality disorder have traits that are:

- Persistent (since early adulthood)
- Pervasive (showing up everywhere—work, love, life)
- Problematic (hurting relationships or themselves)

With this chapter, I hope you can recognise when something deeper might be at play in your relationship—so you can get help, not stay hurt.

1. Borderline Personality Disorder (BPD) aka The Rollercoaster

Core glitch: Fear of abandonment

'She feared I'd leave. In trying to reassure her, I lost myself,' says Sudeep from Daltonganj.

People with BPD live in extremes. Today you're their soulmate, tomorrow you're the villain.

They share nine key traits, but psychologists say that at least five of these are needed for diagnosis.[81]

- Frantic fear of abandonment
- Love-hate, intense relationships
- Rollercoaster moods tied to people

- Impulsive, risky behaviours (sex, shopping, etc.)
- Suicidal thoughts or self-harm (if absent, BPD is less likely)
- Feeling chronically empty
- Shaky self-image
- Explosive, inappropriate anger
- Paranoia or dissociation under stress

BPD is treatable. With therapy and emotional safety, your relationship can get stable again.

2. Narcissistic Personality Disorder (NPD) aka The Selfie

Core glitch: Grandiosity and lack of empathy

'At first, I thought he was confident. Then I realised that everything was about him', says Riya from Bhopal.

People who suffer from NPD are charming and dominating. But if you talk to them about something you need, a time you were hurt or about setting a boundary, you'll either be ignored or attacked. However, underneath the exterior is a fragile ego that can't deal with yours.

NPDs share nine key traits, but psychologists say that at least five of these are needed for diagnosis.

- Inflated self-importance
- Lack of empathy
- Constant need for admiration
- Sense of entitlement
- Manipulative or exploitative behaviour (without this, diagnosis is unlikely)
- Arrogant or dismissive attitude

- Fantasies of success or power
- Belief they're 'special' and elite
- Envy of others, or assuming others envy them

Red flag: If they *never* apologise, always blame you and twist your words into guilt, you'll be emotionally drained dealing with them.

Hope: Change is possible if they want it. Without self-awareness, NPD rarely improves.

Other Disorders

Here are three more common disorders that wreak havoc in relationships—often without getting called out.

3. Obsessive-Compulsive Personality Disorder (OCPD) aka The Perfection Police

They have a rule for everything. Think rigid routines, control-freak energy and zero flexibility. Emotional connection takes a back seat to perfection.

4. Histrionic Personality Disorder (HPD) aka The Drama Queen

Such people have big emotions, loud reactions and a constant need for attention. It's seductive behaviour, but their feelings can be performative.

5. Bipolar Disorder aka The Mood DJ *(Not a personality disorder, but still a relationship rollercoaster)*

One week it's passion, plans and 3 a.m. love poems. The next week brings silence, rage or shutdown. People confuse mood swings with bipolar disorder. But it's a serious disorder that needs medical help.

Love Shouldn't Feel Like a Diagnosis

Before you analyse your partner, analyse yourself. Do you identify with any of these traits? The bravest thing you can do is get help for yourself.

And if you or your partner are constantly walking on eggshells, it's not cardio but a serious red flag.

Up next: Even the healthiest love burns sometimes. What matters is fighting without setting the house on fire.

Do the Damn Thing: Red Flag Radar

Reflect: Here's your Red Flag Radar to spot and handle toxic love like a pro:

- Hot and Cold Vibes: They're your jaan one day, ignoring you the next. It's classic instability.
- Blame Game: They mess up, but you're the villain.
- Control Freak Central: They decide your friends, outfits or career moves without caring what you think.
- Emotional Drain: You're always exhausted from carrying their baggage along with your own.

Act: Talk to a friend or counsellor (try iCall by TISS, free and legit), if the chaos persists. Awareness is your escape hatch.

59
How to Fight Without Burning the Whole Damn Bridge

You don't build courage by avoiding fights.
You build it by surviving them—together.

There is a misconception that couples who seem to have a strong bond don't fight. They just don't fight dirty.

Real relationships are like pressure cookers. Steam builds and emotions rise. And you either learn how to let it out gently … or you have emotional biryani all over the walls.

This chapter is about the art of fighting without blame, arguing without losing the plot and staying close even when it gets loud.

Forged in Fire (aka Fights, Sulks and Late-Night Regrets)

If fighting were an Olympic sport, Megha (my business partner) and I were gold-medal material. We were known for our synchronised sulking and championship-level cold wars. Over fifteen years of running a business, we've shared big fights, silent treatments and plenty of sleepless nights. But we've always had the upmost respect for each other.

I'll never forget the night of her birthday in 2018. We were in a room full of people, but we had had a fight a couple of days ago and hadn't spoken since. But I showed up to her party because I knew that while the fight was temporary, our relationship was forever. She pulled me aside and said with a trembling voice: *'Despite all the fights, please remember you're my closest friend.'*

I'll never forget that, or what she said years later. During the second COVID-19 wave, she lost both her parents within forty-eight hours. And in that fog of grief, she told me: *'If anything happens to me and my husband, I want you to adopt my son.'*

She hadn't asked that of her brother or sisters. She chose me. Our bond went deeper than friendship or partnership. We were family built on on pain, repair and raw honesty.

We all fight with the people we love, but there is never any need for it to turn ugly. That's why we have to fight right.

The Rules of Fighting (Without Breaking Each Other)

1. *Respect is the line you never cross*

Megha and I have yelled at each other and cried, even lashed out. But we never cursed at or humiliated the other. A cruel sentence can never be taken back, and an apology doesn't erase the memory of such encounters.

2. *Silence > Stupidity*

Whenever you are angry with someone and just want to make your thoughts heard loud and clear, my only request is that you shut your mouth. No one has ever said anything wise in the midst of rage. Unless 'Go to hell' is your idea of well-researched travel advice. One of my mentors said it best: 'Zubaan pe taala lagao, warna dil pe taala lag jayega.' Place a lock on your tongue, or your heart will be locked.

3. *Say sorry first. Not because you lost, but because you care*

Waiting for the other person to 'make the first move' is relationship cold war. Be the person to say sorry first. Not because you're wrong, but because you'd rather fix it than win. Your ego isn't a legacy. Let it go.

4. *Ask for help when the fight feels bigger than you*

Some knots can't be untangled alone. Mentors, friends and therapists can help you sort our your feelings. Don't hesitate to approach someone you trust.

5. *Invest before you withdraw*

Relationships are emotional bank accounts. If you don't make deposits, withdrawals aren't possible either. We survived big fights because our deposits—time, trust, care—are way bigger than the withdrawals. Keep investing, daily. That's the only insurance against overdraft.

The Strongest Relationships Are in Constant Repair

Anyone can love when it's easy. But real connection is built in chaos—when you're tired, hurt and still choose each other anyway. Megha and I barely fight now. We still disagree with each other often but we've learnt to listen better, react slower and share our feeling and thoughts.

Some people think having a strong relationship is a matter of luck. It's not. You have to decide to choose each other again and again—after every fight, every pause, every apology. That's the secret to stop relationships breaking down.

Do the Damn Thing: Revisit the Rupture

Reflect: Think of one relationship where a fight nearly ended everything. Was it pride or pain that stopped you from saying sorry?

Act: Send a message to someone you've fought with. Say the first sorry or ask for help. The hardest conversations are the ones that bring us home.

60

Don't Let the Drip Become a Flood

Couples don't break because of big storms. They break because of small, silent leaks no one fixed.

Jatin, my college friend, once told me, 'It wasn't one big fight that ended us. It was the 378 tiny ones we never solved.' He had been married for a long time but got divorced a couple of years ago. Since then, he's often spoken about the mistakes he and his ex-wife made along the way, the biggest of which was allowing their relationship to slowly rust, like an old pipe—corroding from small leaks that neither noticed until the ceiling caved in on them.

It's not always an explosion that ends relationships. Sometimes it is eroded by sarcasm, scrolling and silence. And before the couple knows it, they're two strangers in the house—sharing a Wi-Fi password but not much else.

This chapter is about the real stuff. Not 'why we fight', but what we keep avoiding—and how those little drips destroy love quietly, until it floods everything.

The Fights That Seem Small … But Sting Big

1. *'You Never Listen'*

She talks. He scrolls. She explodes. What it really means: I don't feel heard.

Fix: Put the phone down, look up and say, 'That must've been hard. Tell me more.'

2. *'You Don't Help Me'*

She's doing chores. He's watching reels. She snaps.

What it really means: I'm drowning alone.

Fix: Ask, 'What can I take off your plate today?'

Sometimes marriage is 100-100.

3. *'You're So Cold'*

'You used to be romantic. Now you're robotic.'

What it really means: I miss feeling wanted.

Fix: Speak their love language. Compliment your partner. Give a hug. Say thank you like you mean it.

4. *'The Money Fight'*

One saves. One spends. One sulks.

What it really means: I feel unsafe.

Fix: Do a monthly 'Money Talk' where any kind of judgement is off the table.

5. *'We Never Talk Anymore'*

This spans everything from pillow talk to grocery lists.

What it really means: I miss being friends.

Fix: Ask something fun. 'What's your happiest memory with me?' and take it from there.

6. *'You're So Negative'*

One vents. The other fixes. Everyone's annoyed.

What it really means: Just hold me, don't solve me.

Fix: Say, *'That sucks. I'm here.'* No TED Talk needed.

7. *'Your Family Again?'*

'You always take their side.'

What it really means: Do I come first?

Fix: Say, 'You're my home now. I'll talk to my parents.' Loyalty isn't silent.

8. *'We're Never in the Mood'*

What it really means: Our hearts aren't connecting.

Fix: Build intimacy outside the bedroom. The rest will follow.

9. *'It's Not What You Said—It's How'*

The tone fight is a classic.

What it really means: I feel disrespected.

Fix: Use soft starts. For example, 'I feel …' instead of 'You always …'

10. *'The Little Things'*

'You didn't even notice my haircut.'

What it really means: See me.

Fix: Notice your partner's changes, bring them up in conversation and appreciate them. Love lives in the tiny details.

Mic Drop: Don't Let the Drip Become a Flood

Dr Anjali Chhabria, Mumbai psychiatrist, says, 'Address the drip before it drowns you.' Small fixes save big love. And when ego walks in, love walks out. So, the next time you're mid-fight, don't ask: 'Why are you like this?' Ask: 'How can I understand you better?'

You're not enemies. You're two tired people trying to patch the same damn boat. Stay curious. Stay kind.

Up next: You patched every leak in the relationship. And still, the ceiling caved in. Now what?

Do the Damn Thing: Check In Before You Check Out

Reflect: A flight off by just 1° drifts 1 km every 60 km.

That's what happens to relationships too—small misalignments, ignored long enough, land you in a crash zone. Don't let tiny fights turn into emotional flight diversions.

Act: Think of a fight you have been ignoring. Every fifteen days, do a short check-in with your partner. Ask them:

- 'What made you feel seen or loved recently?'
- 'What's one thing I could've done better?'
- 'Is there anything you're carrying but haven't said out loud yet?'

No judgement. No defence. Just a safe runway for truth.

61

When Letting Go Is Love

Sometimes walking away isn't quitting. It's coming home—to yourself.

I stayed with my wife for nine years. I knew we weren't working out, but I believed that love meant staying—no matter how much it hurt. The cracks were visible; we did it all—fights, silence, draining days, nights where I cried quietly so she wouldn't hear. But still, I stayed.

Because I believed in commitment. Because divorce felt like failure. Because divorce doesn't just mean pain—it means shame.

It took me nearly a decade to understand that staying isn't always strength. Sometimes, it's fear with a good PR team.

Every day in that marriage, I lost a little more of myself—my peace, my humour, my joy. I tried everything: therapy, books, silence, shouting, compromises, retreats. I became a quieter and bitter version of myself.

But nothing helped. We were just wrong for each other. You can't make a plant grow in concrete. You can water it, pray over it, play Mozart to it—but if the soil isn't fertile, nothing will bloom there. That was us: misaligned roots, loud love, but no light.

Divorce Felt Like Death. And Then … Like Air

Despite knowing that we would be happier apart, the day we finally separated didn't feel like a win. It felt like a funeral—of a marriage, of old dreams, of the 'forever' we tried to force. Immediately, the doubts started creeping in. Could I have tried harder?

But then … I slowly came back to life. For the first time in years, I could hear myself again. The noise was gone. And in the silence, I remembered who I was.

First Principle, Boss! Why Letting Go Feels Like Losing a Limb

Your brain hates loss more than it loves peace. As Nobel Prize-winning psychologist Daniel Kahneman showed, 'loss aversion' runs deep—even if that 'loss' is a person who hurt you.[82] So walking away feels like withdrawal, even when it's toxic. That's why the right decision can still feel wrong.

If you're reading this while sitting on the edge—confused, tired, afraid—let me say this: you're not a failure for choosing peace over pain. You're not selfish for wanting a life that doesn't drain you.

Yes, relationships take work. But when work turns into survival, when love starts to feel like emotional debt, it's okay to let go. You're not burning hope. You're making space—for something healthier. Even if that something is just you healing.

Leaving doesn't mean you didn't love enough. It means you finally started loving the one person you forgot: yourself.

Mic Drop: It's Not the Problem, It's the Solution

There's no cure for the common cold. Because it's not the problem. It's the solution—your body's immune system at work. Life works the same way. What looks like a curse might be the cure.

I thought divorce was the problem. Turns out, it was the solution. The door that shut so another one could open. You don't have to suffer just because you once said 'forever'. Loyalty should never feel like a life sentence.

If love starts killing your spirit, walk away. It's an act of love that chooses peace over performance. For them. For you. For the life that's still waiting.

Do the Damn Thing: Choosing Love, Not Longevity

Reflect: Are you staying because there's still a real connection or because you're scared of what leaving might look like?

Act: Try everything—therapy, conversations, hard truths. Let love fight back. But if it keeps feeling like drowning, don't wait for someone to rescue you. Swim to shore. Because saving yourself is the most loving thing you can do.

Bonus: The Relationship Audit

Instructions: Rate each statement from 1 to 5 (1 = Never, 5 = Always). Be honest—this is just for you.

1. Emotional Safety and Trust

- ☐ I feel safe expressing my thoughts and feelings in the relationship.
- ☐ My partner and I are honest with each other, even about hard truths.
- ☐ I trust my partner's intentions, even during disagreements.
- ☐ We resolve conflicts with respect, not blame or insults.

2. Communication and Connection

- ☐ We have meaningful conversations beyond daily logistics.
- ☐ We both listen without interrupting or rushing to fix things.
- ☐ We regularly express appreciation and affection.
- ☐ I feel emotionally seen and heard by my partner.

3. Shared Values and Vision

- [ ] We are aligned on core life values like family, money or lifestyle.
- [ ] We openly discuss differences without judgement.
- [ ] We support each other's goals and growth.
- [ ] I feel we're building something together—not just co-existing.

4. Individuality and Balance

- [ ] I feel free to be myself, without fear of rejection.
- [ ] I have time and space for my own interests and friendships.
- [ ] We respect each other's boundaries and differences.
- [ ] The relationship adds to my life without taking away who I am.

5. Effort and Emotional Intimacy

- [ ] Both of us put effort into nurturing the relationship.
- [ ] We make time to connect, even when life gets busy.
- [ ] Physical affection and emotional intimacy are mutual and fulfilling.
- [ ] I feel we're growing closer over time, not drifting apart.

Your Score and Reflection

90+ points: Your relationship is deeply rooted in connection, effort and mutual respect. Keep nurturing it!

70–89 points: A strong foundation is present, but you may benefit from more intention and conversation.

50–69 points: Some areas need attention. Reflect on the lowest scoring section and start there.

Below 50 points: Time for honest introspection. Use this as a wake-up call, not a judgement on the state of your relationship. Consider open conversations, therapy or deeper self-work.

Modern Kundali: The Thirty-Six-Guna Compatibility Test

Because love isn't astrology. It's psychology with a pulse.

Our grandparents believed in matching horoscopes and thirty-six gunas before deciding if a couple should get married. In fact, a lot of people still do so today, thinking that relationships are more about stars and a cosmic connection than whether the couple is actually compatible. I've compiled a list of eighteen questions that will help you know if you both have it in you to go the distance.

A. Emotional Grounding — Twelve Gunas

1. Attachment Style (Three Gunas)

- Both Secure → **+3**
- One Secure, the other Anxious → **+2**
- One Secure, the other Avoidant → **1**
- One Avoidant, the other Anxious → **–5**

2. Conflict Resolution (Three Gunas)

- Fight fair, repair fast → **+3**
- One repairs, the other avoids → **+2**
- Passive-aggressive / blame cycles → **–1**
- Constant toxic fights, no boundaries → **–5**

3. Trust and Reliability (Two Gunas)

- Consistent and dependable → **+2**
- Flaky sometimes but well-intentioned → **+1**
- Often breaks their word or disappears → **–2**

4. Love Language Awareness (Two Gunas)

- Know and speak each other's love languages → +2
- Try, but not always aligned → +1
- Expect love in our own way and feel unloved often → –1

5. Respecting Each Other's Needs (Two Gunas)

- We both understand what the other truly needs from the relationship → +2
- One tries, the other complains → +1
- Constant mismatch or unmet core needs → –2

B. Relationship Dynamics — Ten Gunas

6. Emotional Health (Three Gunas)

- Emotionally stable, no major unhealed wounds that affect the relationship → **+3**
- Either one is not emotionally stable, gets triggered easily → **-0**
- Neither is emotionally stable → **-3**

7. Sexual Compatibility (Four Gunas)

- Mutual desire, honest feedback → **+4**
- Some mismatch but both are trying → **+2**
- Major gap, one feels shamed or ignored → **–2**

8. Personal Growth Mindset (Three Gunas)

- Takes feedback, wants to grow → **+3**
- Either one is resistant to feedback or growth → **0**
- Both are resistant to feedback or growth → **-3**

C. Life Alignment — Fourteen Gunas

9. Long-Term Vision and Value System (Three Gunas)

- Clear match: kids, city, career, money → **+3**
- Small gaps, open to aligning → **+2**
- Opposing life goals → **–2**

10. Money Mindset (Three Gunas)

- Aligned values, no secrets → **+3**
- Different habits, but transparent → **+1**
- Secretive, controlling or exploitative → **–3**

11. Happiness (Three Gunas)

- Both are generally happy people → **+3**
- One is, the other is not → **0**
- Both are generally unhappy → **–3**

12. Daily Habits and Lifestyle (Two Gunas)

- Sleep, fitness, partying aligned → **+2**
- Some mismatch, but adjusted over time → **+1**
- Regular conflict over routines or boundaries → **–2**

13. Family Interference (Three Gunas)

- Strong boundaries, healthy in-laws → **+3**
- Some parental influence, manageable → **+2**
- Constant meddling or dependence or being completely ignored → **–3**

D. Red Flag Radar — Four Critical Questions

14. Manipulation / Gaslighting (Up to –6)

- Never manipulates, emotionally clear → **0**
- Sometimes blames subtly / guilt-trips → **–2**
- Frequently distorts truth, plays victim → **–6**

15. Ego and Apologies (Up to –4)

- Can own up and apologise → **0**
- Avoids saying sorry but changes behaviour → **–1**
- Never apologises, always blames → **–4**

16. Makes the Partner Feel Small or Unsafe (Up to –4)

- Encouraging, uplifting, safe space → **0**
- Occasional passive criticism → **–2**
- Constant eggshell walking / low self-worth → **–4**

17. Cheating / Loyalty (Up to –6)

- Fully loyal, no sketchy behaviour → **0**
- Past mistake, healed through honesty → **–1**
- Repeats betrayal / secretive chats → **–6**

Final Scoring Guide

Total Score	Compatibility Verdict
31–36	Soulmate Material: It's rare and beautiful, so cherish it.
25–30	Solid Foundation: You are a strong match. Small tweaks to your relationship will lead to magic.
15–24	Caution Zone: Love's there, but some serious leaks need to be fixed.
5–14	High Effort Zone: You'll need a lot of tools along with therapy to rescue this relationship.
Below 5	Red Flag City: It's not love but a pattern you're stuck in. Get out now.

One Last Thing Before You Panic

This score isn't fixed. It can grow just like you. Don't use it to blame each other. Instead, talk, listen and repair.

Strong relationships are built every day. Start now.

Before You Move On ...

Relationships are the heartbeat of a meaningful life. Great relationships, like health or success, need time, effort and emotional honesty.

You've reflected, assessed and grown. Now, take these insights and show up. Be more present, aware and loving. Because the next chapter of your life deserves stronger bonds and deeper connections.

SECTION 5

HEALTH

FUEL FIRST

INSIDE SCIENCE

TRAIN SMART

TRANSFORM

Inspired by Lord Dhanvantari

Long ago, when gods and demons teamed up to churn the cosmic ocean for hidden treasures, the first thing to pop out was poison. They kept going, and then out walked the god of Ayurveda—Dhanvantari, an avatar of Vishnu, holding a pot of amrit. The nectar of immortality was the real jackpot.

Health beats every other treasure. This section is about building that treasure daily—through habits so small they feel ordinary, yet protect you like the nectar itself.

62

Health is Not Rocket Science ... Or Is It?

The food you eat is either fuel ... or a slow-motion suicide note.

—Probably not your mom, but should've been

Everyone says the road to good health is simple: eat veggies, avoid junk food and sleep early. Then why are so many smart, educated people still tired, bloated, foggy or diabetic?

Because health is simple in theory—and a giant mind maze in practice. If staying fit was truly as easy as 'eat less, move more', dieticians could get certified during a tea break, and fitness trainers could qualify by doing jumping jacks on Zoom. But real health is like your college crush—mysterious, layered and never as straightforward as it seems.

The Illusion of Knowing

I've been in the health game for nearly two decades—I built a nutrition company, took courses, worked with thousands of clients and wrote books on the subject. And the biggest truth I've learnt is that the more you study health, the more you realise you know nothing.

That humility keeps me curious. Let me show you what I mean.

Truth Bombs Incoming

1. *Walking ≠ Weight Loss*

A forty-year-old CEO walked 10,000 steps daily, but his sugar levels didn't reduce. Why? His plate was the real villain. Walking is cardio, not a miracle. Depending on your speed, diet and metabolism, it might be doing almost nothing to your body. Plus, weight loss is more about eating right and not the number of steps you walk.

2. *Ghar Ka Khana Isn't Automatically Healthy*

'Beta, home food is best.' There will hardly be a mother in India who didn't say this to their kids. Yes, home food is safer, but that doesn't automatically make it balanced. Most Indian diets are overloaded with carbs—roti, rice, potato—and painfully low in protein. We need to include more protein in Indian diets that isn't dal. Because dal is not enough. Protein is a crucial building block for our bodies, and is essential for the growth and repair of cells, muscles, bones and tissue. Eat more of what you need—whether it's cooked at home or in a healthy manner outside.

3. *One Person's Superfood = Another's Hospital Bill*

Our bodies react differently to different foods and diets. The ketogenic diet is popular because it involves consuming a very low amount of carbohydrates and replacing them with fat to help your body burn fat for energy. One person may lose 5 kilos on the diet, while another can get gallstones because of the high fat intake. Your body is not a Google Sheet. It's a living, breathing, hormone-fuelled, sleep-deprived, stress-soaked ecosystem. Food is deeply personal. Following someone else's diet plan is like wearing their underwear. It might fit, but will never be as comfortable as yours.

Health = Learning + Unlearning

Most of the damage caused to our bodies isn't from junk food.

It's from junk beliefs.

- '*Fat is bad.*' (Sugar's the real villain.)
- '*Dal is enough.*' (Only if you're a cow.)
- '*XYZ is unhealthy.*' (Use Instagram to chill, not to panic.)

We carry silent scripts in our bodies—passed down like family heirlooms.

So health isn't just knowing what to do but about questioning what you've been told since you were five.

Mic Drop: Your Body Isn't Lying. Your Beliefs Might Be

Health isn't rocket science. But it's not toddler maths either. It's messy, contextual, hormonal, emotional and highly personal. It's less about perfection and more about attention to what your body is really saying. You also need to start asking better questions. And the first one is this:

Are your taste buds truly yours… Or were they hijacked?

Because the real villain in this story might be sitting in your snack drawer.

Let's find out next.

Do the Damn Thing: Thank Your Body

Reflect: What has your body done for you today that you didn't thank it for?

Act (Meditation): Walk barefoot on grass or the floor at home. Walk slowly and silently. With each step, say in your mind: 'I am alive. I am here. Thank you.'

63

Why You Crave Pizza More Than Bananas (Hint: Blame Santa)

> *'Your body is not programmed to crave junk food. It was trained to.'*
>
> *—Michael Pollan*

> *'I don't enjoy healthy food. I love junk food.'*

We all love junk food, and even tell ourselves that we just can't resist it. Healthy food just doesn't match up. But the surprising thing is that we were born to enjoy healthy food like bananas, berries and bhindi. It's just that our taste buds got kidnapped by a gang of marketers in red ties and expensive suits. Don't believe me? Let me show you how.

Why You Crave Pizza More Than Bananas

Give people two options: pizza or banana. Ninety per cent will pick pizza. Now give the same options to our cousins, monkeys (remember, we share 99 per cent of our DNA). Banana wins every single time.

Let's say you're more 'evolved' than a monkey. Then answer this: what would your nani pick? A banana. Without a second thought. For years, humans craved natural foods—not because of discipline but by design. So, what changed in the last fifty years? One word: marketing.

The Santa Claus Brainwash (Yes, Really)

You've probably heard of Pavlov's dog experiment: ring a bell → feed the dog → dog drools. Eventually, just ring the bell, and the dog still drools. That's called conditioning.

Now watch how Coca-Cola pulled a Pavlov on your brain. Before 1931, Santa Claus was skinny, creepy and sometimes even wore brown. Then the marketing guys at Coke said, 'Nah, make him chubby and cheerful. In our red and white.' A new Santa was born. Happy Santa.[83]

Now when you see red and white, you think joy, gifts, sugar, nostalgia … and Coke. They didn't sell you a drink. They sold you a feeling. And companies do the same with junk food.

'But I Just Crave Chips, Bro …'

Let's break that myth: cravings = lack of willpower. Nope. Cravings = cleverly engineered brain hijack.

Food scientists design chips, biscuits and colas to be addictive, the perfect cocktail of salt, sugar and fat. We fall in love with the crunch, aroma and colours. Even the packaging is planned like a thriller movie. Add some Netflix, a little dopamine … and boom—you're Pavlov's dog with a delivery app.

The average Indian child sees mostly junk on their screens. A 2021 study found that *88 per cent* of food ads on children's channels were for high-fat, high-salt, high-sugar foods.[84] There are no ads for fruits or vegetables. And after watching just five minutes of junk-food ads, they consume an extra 130 calories—that's one chocolate bar every day.[85]

Yes, junk food is tempting but it's possible to reclaim your taste buds. Healthy food isn't boring. You've just been brainwashed to think it is. It's time to untrain your tongue.

- ✔ Cravings aren't real—they're rehearsed.
- ✔ Food isn't 'fun' or 'sad'—it's just fuel.
- ✔ Health is your *default*, not your punishment.

The good news is that taste buds can reset. In two to three weeks of consuming healthier food, it starts tasting really good. You just need to fight past the first fake cravings.

Mic Drop: The Villain Isn't Your Tongue. It's Your Triggers

Start noticing the triggers. TV = popcorn. Stress = chocolate. Boredom = Swiggy. We are all guilty of this. Your tongue isn't the problem, what you associate with it is. Change those … and you win.

Up next: What if I told you healthy eating doesn't mean eating less, but eating more? Let's flip the script.

64

I Got Six-Pack Abs Without Quitting Chocolate, Booze or Life

'Moderation in all things is the secret to health.'

—Ayurveda Sutra

Let's start with a weird science trick. Take an empty glass and try removing the air from it. Tough, right? Now pour water in, and the air is gone.

That's exactly how your cravings work. Instead of fighting them, you need to fill them—with better stuff.

But most people do the opposite. They go cold turkey and give up food with sugar and grease. Suddenly, food becomes Tinder—all red flags and regret.

And guess what? The more you say, 'I can't have this', the more your brain starts moaning like a dramatic ex.

Forbidden = irresistible.[86]

Ask Adam and Eve. They probably weren't hungry. They were just told not to eat the apple.

Add First. Subtract Later (If At All)

Instead of fighting cravings, confuse them. Add a handful of nuts. A cup of buttermilk. That sad cucumber. Do it before the chips show up like toxic relatives.

Your body doesn't want junk—it wants satisfaction. Real food = real signals to your brain to calm down. This shows us that you don't need a strict break-up with food, just better boundaries.

Yes, food is not the villain. 'I'm scared of potatoes. Cashews make you fat. Sugar is basically cocaine' are common topics of conversation. But it's food, not a mafia boss. We've been brainwashed by influencers with twelve-pack abs and zero empathy who make food look like it's out to kill you.

But here's the truth: food isn't evil. Our relationship with it is toxic.

My Abs. My Rules

On 1 Jan 2024, I made a wild resolution: I would get six-pack abs in five months without giving up any food.

That meant, I ...

- Ate meat daily
- Had chocolate or ice cream every single day
- Drank alcohol weekly (strictly for hydration purposes, of course)
- Took holidays every month
- Attended a Marwari wedding (aka the boss of overeating)

And still at the end of five months, I had 10 per cent body fat and abs so sharp they could slice gajar halwa.

I learnt that building abs don't require you to torture yourself. You need strategy, a little science and a plate that's smarter and not sadder.

So How TF Did I Pull That Off?

I made simple swaps and chose smart portions.

- 500ml cola → 150ml
- Full chocolate bar → 2 small squares
- Big bag of chips → 30g pack

I was better each day than the one before. Also, find smarter alternatives:

- Dark chocolate over regular one
- Zero-sugar ice cream
- Roasted snacks over fried
- Tandoori food over fried stuff
- High protein over carb-heavy

Being healthy doesn't require you to quit food. You just need to quit the all-or-nothing belief.

Mic Drop: Food = Joy. Not Jail

Food is a celebration. It's mangoes in May. Ghar ka khana after a flight. That one bite of mithai at a wedding when the DJ plays *Chaiyya Chaiyya*.

Food is not punishment or poison. It's a memory. It's medicine. So instead of asking, 'What should I cut out?' try asking, 'What can I add that my body will secretly high-five me for?'

Because sometimes, the problem may be that your daily plate—dal, chawal, roti, sabzi—is missing half the nutrients your body's begging for. Let's decode that next.

Exercise: Eat More, Not Less

Reflect: Which healthy food groups are missing from your meals—fruits, proteins, greens, good fats?

Act: This week, add *one* new healthy item to your plate every day—without cutting anything out.

65

Is Your Indian Thali Healthy … or a Hidden Diabetes Bomb?

'Let food be thy medicine and medicine be thy food.'

—Hippocrates (way ahead of his time, clearly)

It is a truth universally acknowledged, that every desi auntie polishing off three rotis and a spoon of sabzi will say, 'Indian food is the healthiest!'

Let's cut the halwa and get honest.

A typical Indian thali today looks like this:

- South Indian: A hill of rice, a dry lake of sambar and a *lost island of vegetables*.
- North Indian: Just swap rice with rotis. And maybe add some ghee so it looks 'healthy'.

It's basically a carb tsunami. Protein? It's on a missing person poster. Veggies? Doing cameo roles like a junior artiste in a Karan Johar film.

But still, we chant that our food is the best. If that's true, why are 15 crore Indians dealing with diabetes or prediabetes? Why are we called the diabetes capital of the world?

Because the killer is hiding in plain sight—soft, warm and round—like that third roti you didn't need, but ate anyway. A 2020 study by leading researchers compared Indian diets to the global gold standard (the EAT-Lancet Reference Diet).[87] The findings are kind of embarrassing:

- Protein intake was just 6–8 per cent (vs the ideal 29 per cent)
- Fruit and vegetables? Barely half of what's recommended
- Carbs (mainly rice/wheat) made up 60–70 per cent of total calories

Basically, our meals include too many carbs, too little protein and fruits treated like garnish.

The Real Plot Twist on Your Plate

Here's what most of us eat:

- *Too many carbs*: Roti → rice → more roti → feeling sleepy → more rice
- *Too little protein*: Paneer and dal are treated like side characters.
- *Hardly any veggies*: One spoon for colour, not for nutrition.

Your thali is not unhealthy because it's Indian. It's unhealthy because it's imbalanced.

The Desi Thali, But Make It Healthy

Let's build a plate your body (and future blood sugar reports) will love:

- **⅓ vegetables** (raw, cooked, stir-fried, even air-fried)
- **⅓ protein** (dal, curd, paneer, eggs, meat, sprouts—pick your fighter)
- **⅓ carbs** (roti, rice, millets—preferably not all three at once)

Eating this may feel weird at first. Like pineapple on pizza. Or Akshay Kumar doing a gutkha ad.

But give it a week. Your bloating will vanish, energy will spike and the mirror will smirk back at you.

Myth: 'Our Ancestors Ate the Same Thali!'

Yeah. And they also:

- Walked a lot every day
- Slept like babies
- Had no Netflix or traffic
- Didn't eat maida momos at 1 a.m.
- Drank more milk than your gym bro's protein shake

So no, your ancestors weren't superhumans. They just lived cleaner, moved more and didn't have sugar in everything.

Mic Drop: Better Plate = Better Fate

Fixing your plate won't just change your weight. It'll change your energy, skin, mood and sleep. (And maybe even your parents' cholesterol report.)

But wait—even a healthy plate can backfire if you're not careful. We'll spill that dal in the next chapter.

Do the Damn Thing: Make Your Plate Healthier

Reflect: Does your plate have mostly carbs like rice or roti, with just a little dal or veggies on the side?

Act: Flip the ratio. For every roti, add a full bowl of dal or curd. Add veggies too. Try pouring a small portion of rice into a bowl of dal and eat it like a broth. The simple tweak will give your health a big upgrade.

For a moment, drop the nostalgia.

Drop the patriotism.

Think from first principles: is your thali serving your health?

66

Chew Like a Monk. Not a Machine

'Drink your food. Eat your drink.'

—Mahatma Gandhi

(who would have thought him a nutrition influencer)

What if I told you there's one habit that can improve your digestion, boost metabolism, reduce acidity and even help you lose weight—without changing your diet, without adding workouts and without buying some overpriced smoothie made of spinach and sadness?

Just one thing: chew. Yes, that boring, underrated, background task your jaw does as you watch reels.

The Speed-Eater Syndrome

Meet Sameer. He finishes a full plate of food in just eight minutes flat—while watching reels. By 8:15 p.m., he's unbuttoning his jeans, and by 8:20, he's Googling: 'Why am I bloated after eating healthy food?'

Sameer hasn't learnt the basics of eating food.

Myth: Digestion starts in your stomach.

Truth: It starts in your damn mouth.

Chewing breaks down food, which releases enzymes and makes nutrients easier to absorb. That's what saves your gut from a full-blown gas concert.

Why Your Jaw Might Be the Real Fitness Coach

1. *Chewing prevents overeating.*

Your stomach takes twenty minutes to send a 'Bro, I'm full' signal to your brain. But most of us finish eating in just twelve minutes, which means you're two rotis over quota before your brain even logs in.

2. *It improves digestion.*

Chewing = smaller particles = less drama for your digestive system.

Which means less bloating, less acidity and fewer burps of regret.

3. *It helps you eat less … without trying.*

Slow eaters consume fewer calories because they're not shoving food like it's a speed date.

Fun stat: Fast eaters are 115 per cent more likely to be obese than slow eaters.[88] Even Buddha knew this and told his monks: 'Eat in silence.' This means no talking and scrolling. Just chew fully and mindfully. Because the way you eat = the way you live.

Slow chewing = calm mind.

Fast chewing = fast-forwarding through life (and your digestion).

So yeah… chewing is therapy. Just cheaper.

Okay, but how slow is slow?

My grandma had once told me to chew my food thirty-two times—one for every tooth I had. There's no need to do that. Instead:

- 15–20 chews per bite (or until it feels like soup)
- Curd = quick
- Roti, sabzi = chew it like you love it
- And yes, your nani was right: 'Don't talk while eating.'
- Put your spoon down between bites
- Use a smaller spoon (or chopsticks if you're feeling exotic)
- Make each roti last five minutes (challenge accepted?)
- Avoid deep conversations at dinner—or risk swallowing your opinions with your aloo

Up next: Think you know calories? Let's mess with that number you've been chasing (and miscounting).

67

Calories Count, but Context Slaps Harder

'Eat less, move more.'

—Every Instagram fitness guru ever

The key to good health, apparently, is to eat less and move more. Sounds simple, right? But if it really worked, half the country wouldn't be Googling 'how to lose belly fat without doing anything'.

People don't gain weight because they're lazy.

They do so because they don't understand one magic word—calories.

Wait, WTF Is a Calorie?

Imagine your body is a car. A calorie = petrol. No fuel = no motion. Too much fuel? You're just leaking everywhere.

Technically, 1 calorie is the energy needed to raise the temperature of 1 gram of water by 1°C. Cool. That's useless information.

Here's what you actually need to know: Calories = energy. Too much = weight gain. Too little = weight loss. Just right = Goldilocks zone (or as your Kalpana didi says, 'Bilkul perfect').

Your Daily Calorie Budget = TDEE

TDEE is Total Daily Energy Expenditure. Basically, it's how many calories your body burns each day for every activity you perform—from sleeping to scrolling to sulking over your ex.

It's made of:

- BMR (Basal Metabolic Rate): Calories to stay alive. (Think: breathing, blinking)
- Activity: Walking, gymming, chasing your dog
- Thermic Effect of Food: Yes, even chewing needs calories (You're basically burning fat while biting.)

Quick hack to calculate your daily burn:

- Men → weight (kg) × 24
- Women → weight (kg) × 22

  That's your BMR.

Now multiply with BMR with …

- 1.2, if you have a sedentary lifestyle
- 1.4, if you are lightly active
- 1.6, if you are moderately active
- 1.8, if you are very active
- 2, if you are an athlete

That's your TDEE.

If you want to lose fat, eat 15–20 per cent below it. And if you are looking to gain muscle, go 10–15 per cent above that.

Calories in Common Foods = Plot Twists Incoming

- 1 g protein = 4 calories
- 1 g carb = 4 calories
- 1 g fat = 9 calories
- 1 g alcohol = 7 calories (yes, your 'light' beer is lying to you)

This is why fried food + booze = calorie chaos. And here's the kicker: one slice of cake = ~350 calories, 30-minute jog = ~200 calories. You can't outrun a bad diet. Unless you're Usain Bolt on Red Bull (oh, that's another 160 calories).

But calories aren't the villain. Confusion is. Weight gain isn't about the presence of calories—it's about excess calories, especially from sugar bombs, junk food and the 'just one bite' biryani rounds. And before you say, 'But roti and cookie have the same calories,' remember that whole food calories = fuel. Junk food calories = chaos.

Let's Play Calorie Confessions

Round 1: What has more calories? A shiny apple or 200 ml cola? Answer: Apple. (Yeah, but guess which one your liver prefers.)

Round 2: What's worse for your body? 100 calories of cauliflower vs 100 calories of ice cream? Even a sixth grader knows this. But somehow, some adults still argue with MyFitnessPal data that both are the same.

Why 'Calories In = Calories Out' Is BS

Your body isn't a calculator. It's a full-blown chemistry lab.

Example: 1 g sugar = 4 calories; 1 g protein = 4 calories

The numbers are the same but the effects are different.

- Sugar: spikes insulin, stores fat, ruins mood
- Protein: builds muscle, burns during digestion, keeps you full (and full of yourself)

And what about fibre, which also has 4 calories? It is technically a carb, but undigested. It just sweeps your gut like Swachh Bharat in action. Fibre is the only thing that deserves negative calories and a Padma Shri. So yeah, the old logic of 'calorie in = calorie out' is a bit ... outdated.

Context Is King

Food is more than just calories. Let's break it down like a Bollywood masala movie:

1. Chemicals: Zero calories, but your gut throws a dhamaal.
2. Nutrients: Calories don't list vitamins, but your body's filmi maa notices what's missing.
3. Food quality: Chips vs. almonds? One does Bharatnatyam, the other betrayal.
4. Hormones: PCOS? Thyroid? Your body listens to chemistry, not calculators. *Yeh love story calorie se nahi, hormone se likhi gayi hai.* Hence, a person suffering from thyroid or PCOS gains weight, despite eating the same calories as before.

Calories matter. But context matters more. Would you spend your money on fireworks or gold? It's the same with calories. Don't waste them on empty pleasures—invest them in food that actually loves you back.

Calories may not be evil. But carbs? They've been accused of every crime from belly fat to heartbreak. Let's settle the debate next.

68
Cut Crap, Not Carbs

'The problem isn't carbs. It's what we've done to them.'
—Michael Pollan, a food writer who probably eats better than all of us

The moment someone decides to lose weight, what's the first thing they ditch? Carbs.

But here's the truth no keto bro wants to admit: yes, you can lose weight by cutting carbs. But can you survive the loss without turning into a cranky toddler? That's the real test.

Carbs aren't evil. They're just misunderstood. Your brain, thyroid and even your mood need them. The key isn't cutting carbs, it's choosing better ones—and not overdosing.

Why Your Body Actually Loves Carbs

- Carbs = Energy. They fuel walking, thinking, breathing … and even heartbreak scrolling.

- They support your thyroid, mood and electrolyte balance.
- They make your food colourful and fun.
- Fibre—a carb cousin—keeps your gut clean and your toilet visits regular.
- Ditching carbs completely? That just leads to cravings, mood swings and eventually … a samosa relapse.

Even Ayurveda loves carbs—it called rice and ghee the food of the gods. One study showed women who cut carbs for three days ended up eating ~40 per cent more calories on Day 4.[89]

Because willpower has limits.

So Where Do Carbs Go Wrong?

There are two problems.

Refined carbs are the real villains. Not all carbs.

Our diet is dominated by carbs. You can't make a winning team with eleven Virat Kohlis. You need balance.

Excess and refined carbs spike your blood sugar, pump out insulin (aka fat-storage mode) and shut down fat-burning. That means belly fat, thigh fat, double chin—all delivered faster than your Zomato order.

Here's a hack to check whether carbs are healthy or not: check the fibre content of the food. The more fibre it has, the more your body will love it. If it has less fibre, it crashes your system faster.

How to Eat Carbs Without Becoming a Potato

- **Pair carbs with protein.**
  Chhole + rice. Dal + roti.
  This slows down sugar release and keeps you full longer.
- **Watch portions.**
  Your plate doesn't have to be a rice mountain.

(Flip to the 'Know Your Plate' chapter for ninja-level tips.)

- **Go whole, not hollow.**
  Brown rice > white rice. Whole wheat roti > white bread. Basically: fibre in, drama out.

Let's Bust Some Carb Myths (With Facts, Not Fear)

Myth 1: Bananas make you fat.

Truth: Jyoti from Bhubaneshwar once told me she hadn't touched a banana in two years because it was 'fattening'. Turns out, it was just Instagram advice gone rogue.

One banana = ~100 calories + potassium + fibre. Eat it, don't fear it.

Myth 2: Brown bread is good for weight loss.

Truth: A lot of brown bread is just white bread in a costume (thanks to added caramel). Choose whole wheat bread.

Myth 3: Dal, rajma and chana cause weight gain.

Truth: Nope. They're full of protein. They might cause gas, not fat.

Myth 4: Carbs = Fat

Truth: Carbs hold water, not fat: 1 g of carbs = 3–4 g of water. Cut carbs from your diet, and you lose water. Eat carbs, and you gain it back. It's water weight, not betrayal.

Myth 5: Potatoes are bad.

Truth: 100 g potato = 24 g carbs. 100 g dal = 63 g carbs. 100 g brown rice = 76 g carbs. Surprise! Potatoes have fewer carbs than your so-called 'healthy' foods. Plus, they provide vitamin C, potassium and barely any fat. Basically, it's the sabzi ka superstar, not the villain.

Carbs = Chaos? Not Really

Carbs are not your enemy. Ultra-processed, low-fibre junk is. The goal isn't to cancel roti; it's to stop treating cookies like lunch. So don't ghost carbs—just friendzone the processed ones.

Up next: Protein—The Unsung Hero You've Been Ignoring Since Class 6.

69

Protein: The Most Underrated, Friend-Zoned Nutrient Ever

You don't get strong by chance. You get strong by protein.

'Why should I take protein, bro? I am not competing for Mr. World.'
'And, hello, I am a girl. I want great skin, not Hulk arms.'

If I had a scoop of whey for every time I heard this, or its variations, I'd have better biceps—and better patience. Thanks to bro-science and Bollywood, we think protein's only for sweaty dudes in stringers, grunting like they're giving birth at Gold's Gym. But the truth is that protein isn't just for muscles. It's for survival. And yes, ladies, that includes you too.

Protein isn't just for bodybuilders; it's also great for protecting bones, developing our brains, getting better hair, boosting immunity, and balancing hormones. In short—it's for everyone. Protein is like that overachiever who gets friend-zoned while fries get all the action.

Protein is the building block of your body. Every cell in your body needs protein. Protein builds everything—from your brain cells to your booty. You're literally made of the stuff. It's not just a supplement; it's your skeleton's BFF. Hair fall, random cravings and mood swings that make you wanna punch a wall? Your body's basically screaming: 'Send protein, you idiot, not more chai!'

Approximately 73 per cent of Indians are protein-deficient, according to an Indian Market Research Bureau survey.[90] Few of us grew up knowing the importance of protein in a diet. We gave protein a side role on our plates—and then wondered why our body's performance sucked.

Protein Isn't a Gym Thing. It's a Life Thing

Protein isn't a luxury, it's a daily essential. Every adult—even if they've never stepped inside a gym—needs 0.8 to 1.2 g of protein per kilogram of body weight just to function well.[91] That's like needing oxygen—not for a marathon but to survive every day. That means a 60-kg person needs about 60 g of protein daily. Most Indians barely touch 30 g.

You need more than that—1.2–2.5 g/kg of body weight—if you're working out, losing weight or trying to grow muscle. If you don't pay attention or dismiss this need for protein, you'll likely fall short—and you won't even know it until fatigue, poor recovery, hair fall or constant hunger show up like unwanted relatives.

Not All Proteins Are Made Equal

Imagine comparing a Ranbir Kapoor movie to a Govinda classic.

Sure, both are films, but the quality, vibe and results are very different.

Similarly, protein sources vary in quality:

- Animal proteins (eggs, fish, chicken, milk, paneer): They are complete proteins because they contain all the nine essential amino acids.
- Plant proteins (dal, chana, rajma, soy): They are usually incomplete. But when you mix them smartly (dal + rice, roti + chana, bread + peanut butter), they become complete.

Also, absorption matters in:

- 1 g protein from milk is almost fully absorbed.
- 1 g from dal? Around 50-75 per cent.

But a bowl of dal with a roti? That's a power couple. Try to have them in the same proportion.

Protein also helps you lose weight. In one study, folks who upped their protein intake (30 per cent of their diet) dropped 5 kg in twelve weeks and ate 450 calories less—no kale smoothies, no cult-like fasting, just more protein.[92]

Truth Bombs Incoming

Now, let's bust some protein myths.

Myth: Too much protein will damage my kidneys.

Fact: Only if you already have a kidney issue or you consume more than 300 g a day. For healthy people, protein is safe—and necessary.

Myth: I can't get enough protein as a vegetarian.

Fact: You absolutely can. But you need to be smart about combining foods—like soya + rice, or dal + roti + paneer. My top protein picks for vegetarians are paneer, tofu, soya, cheese, peanuts, protein powders, high protein varieties of regular food (dahi, bread, muesli, dosa batter).

Myth: Protein will make me bulky.

Fact: This is like saying owning a football will make you Cristiano Ronaldo. Women don't have enough testosterone to turn into Hulk—unless they're hiding a beard and a secret lab.

Myth: Protein supplements are unhealthy or 'unnatural'.

Fact: That's like saying grinding peanuts makes peanut butter unnatural.

Or boiling milk makes it toxic. Whey protein = Concentrated milk protein. Paneer = Solid milk protein. They're literally Karan-Arjun—*Dono ek hi maa ke bachche hain … doodh ki*! Think of whey/plant protein as your lazy hack—the Tinder of nutrition. Swipe, scoop, shake and you're done.

What to Eat: Easy Protein Sources

Food Item	Protein per 100g
Egg (1 whole)	6g
Chicken/Fish	20–25g
Paneer	18g
Soya chunks	52g
Dal (cooked)	5g
Milk and curd	3g
Whey protein	20–25g per scoop

Protein Is Your Life Insurance Policy

Whether you lift dumbbells or just lift grocery bags, your body needs protein. They give you energy, clarity and less hair on your pillow. Protein's got your back about almost everything related to good nutrition.

So the next time someone asks, 'Why are you eating eggs if you're not working out?', just smile and say, 'I'm building a healthy life, not just biceps.' Because protein is a life insurance policy—without the paperwork.

Now, we have talked about carbs and protein. What about fat? Does fat make us fat? Let's deep-dive.

70

Dear Fat, I'm Sorry I Judged You

'Removing fat from your diet is like removing oil from an engine. You might feel proud. But it's gonna break.'

—Some wise nutrition rebel

There was a time I looked at ghee like it was a crime scene. Butter? No way. Cheese? It was temptation from hell. But low-fat curd? Yes, please.

Like every confused 90s kid, I was told that fat was the devil. So, I proudly ate 'low-fat' everything … until I realised I was just swapping fat for sugar and chemicals. Of course, I wasn't getting fitter. I was just experiencing more mood swings.

Turns out, fat was never the villain. It just had bad PR.

Why Fat Deserves an Apology

We all need fat in our bodies. It isn't optional. Your brain is 60 per cent fat.[93] Cutting out fat to get healthy is like skipping petrol to make your car lighter. Fat helps you:

- Make hormones (yes, even the ones that decide if you're hangry or flirty)
- Absorb vitamins like A, D, E, K
- Keep your skin glowing and joints happy
- Stay full so you don't end up elbow-deep in a chips packet at midnight.

Still think fat is the enemy? Your brain would like to unsubscribe from that nonsense.

Good Fat vs Bad Fat: Let's Build Your Dream Team

If your kitchen was an IPL team:

Good fats (Monounsaturated Fatty Acids and Polyunsaturated Fatty Acids) = the all-rounders. They are found in olive oil, nuts, seeds, avocado, fish and help your heart, brain, mood, skin—basically your whole vibe.

Trans fats = the cheaters that are found in fried foods, biscuits, margarine, namkeen. They raise bad cholesterol, lower good cholesterol and ruin your health.

Saturated fats = the misunderstood players that are found in ghee, butter, coconut oil and the like. They are neither angels nor villains. We just need to consume them in moderation. Think Virat Kohli at a buffet: he'll show up, take a few bites and then leave before he reaches the dessert section.

Stop Falling for These Fat Myths

Myth 1: Fat makes you fat.

Truth: Sugar, refined carbs and overeating make you fat. Good fats help you feel full and even burn fat.

Myth 2: Low-fat = healthy.

Truth: It often means high sugar + shady chemicals. That *'low-fat'* chocolate yogurt? You might as well eat a Dairy Milk bar and cry honestly.

Myth 3: Cheese is unhealthy.

Truth: Cheese is protein, calcium and joy as long as you don't overdo it and keep portion size in mind.

Myth 4: Ghee is unhealthy.

Truth: Ghee aids digestion, improves joint strength, adds glow to your skin … and soul to your paratha.

1–3 teaspoons a day = fine. 1 tablespoon per bite = hello, cholesterol.

The Cooking Oil Cheat Sheet

I've made you a quick cheat sheet for cooking oils from high heat to none. Choosing the right oils for the right kind of cooking method ensures you make healthy choices.

- High heat cooking: Ghee, mustard oil, peanut oil
- Medium heat: Butter, sesame oil
- Low heat/salads: Olive oil (cold-pressed), flaxseed oil, walnut oil

Avoid refined oils as much as possible. Choose cold-pressed or kachhi ghani oils. Your body deserves first-class fuel, not leftover fryer oil from a roadside dhaba.

But how much fat do we actually need? Desk job + Netflix lifestyle → 3–4 tsp oil/day. Workout + 10k steps squad → 4–6 tsp/day. And that's just visible oil. Don't forget the invisible fat in nuts, seeds, eggs, fish and more.

Mic Drop: Fat Isn't Bad. Your Info Was

Next time someone says, 'I'm on a zero-fat diet,' just pat their back and say, 'Cool. Say hi to hair fall, dull skin and hormone chaos.' Because fat isn't junk. Fat is fuel—for your brain and your biryani.

Now that we've made peace with fat, let's meet the body part that decides your mood more than your brain. Yup, your gut.

71

You're Not Alone—You're 100 Trillion

Your gut is not just where food goes. It's where your health begins.

There's a colony of 100 trillion beings inside you. They are working silently, day and night, in perfect harmony. Their mission? To keep their world alive.

But they don't operate alone. They rely on a powerful machine to feed them, clean them and keep them running. In return, they heal the machine, defend it and balance it.

But what happens when the machine turns rogue? Maybe it sends the wrong fuel or forgets about them? Then the colony stops helping, and the machine begins to collapse—from the inside.

It sounds like science fiction, doesn't it? But it's not. That colony is real. It's your gut microbiome. And the machine they depend on is you. Feed them well, and they boost your mood, digestion and immunity. Feed them junk, and they quietly rebel.

They're the real boss of your body. You're just the host. So, are you feeding your inner colony, or letting your system rot from the core?

Gut Feelings Are Real AF

You think you have free will? Your gut bugs might be voting for you. Craving sugar? It might be the sugar-addicted bacteria begging for a hit. Feeling low for no reason? Could be a gut imbalance messing with your serotonin.

Science now calls your gut the second brain—it has over 100 million neurons.[94] Ayurveda called it Agni—your digestive fire. And both agree that if your gut's off, everything is off. Mood swings, skin breakouts, stubborn fat, low energy, anxiety, insomnia aren't just lifestyle issues. They're gut issues in disguise.

And your gut doesn't just digest food. It digests emotions. So, if you're stressed, guess who else is stressed? Yep, the bacteria.

When Rats Prove More than Therapists

Still not convinced your gut runs the show? Let's talk science.

Researchers at Washington University in St. Louis, led by Dr Jeffrey Gordon, did a wild experiment in 2013.[95] They took gut bacteria from two people—one lean, one obese—and transferred them into two rats. They were given the same food in the same cage. After a few days, the results were a surprise.

Obese gut = Obese rat
Lean gut = Lean rat

Then the experiment was repeated to test for depression. When they gave rats gut bacteria from depressed humans, they started showing actual signs of depression—less movement, less curiosity and classic 'giving up' behaviour.[96] Scientists call this the **gut–brain axis**, a two-way emotional highway. Your gut bugs can change your mood, your motivation and even how you respond to stress. Your gut might be silently making you fat. Or sad. Or both.

Gut Politics: Monks vs Gangsters

Think of your gut like a city. Good bacteria = peaceful monks. Bad bacteria = hungry gangsters. Your food = their fuel.

When you eat clean, fibre-rich food, the monks take over. And when you binge on junk, the gangsters riot. It's a case of full-blown gut politics.

If you want a peaceful gut, you need to feed the right crowd.

Here's your gut-friendly grocery gang:

- Prebiotics (garlic, onion, banana, asparagus): These feed the good guys.
- Probiotics (curd, homemade pickles, fermented foods): These *are* the good guys.
- Fibre-rich foods (fruits, veggies, nuts, seeds, whole grains): Bacteria playground.
- Water: Because a constipated gut is a grumpy gut.
- Stress management: Because anxiety nukes your gut faster than Coke and chips.

With expert advice, you can also explore the following products/ supplements: L-glutamine, apple cider vinegar, digestive enzymes and Betaine HCL.

But I'd recommend that you start with food first and only opt for supplements when they are not enough.

You're not eating for one. You're feeding 100 trillion invisible guests. Treat them well … or they'll riot from the inside.

Your gut is your factory, your therapist, your immune army and your emotional Wi-Fi. You can't ghost it, binge on nonsense and expect to glow. Because in the end, health doesn't start in the gym. It starts in the gut.

Speaking of the gym, let's discuss exercise next.

Do the Damn Thing: Reset. Rebuild. Repair.

Reflect: Are you paying attention to what your gut needs? Or just eating whatever's easy?

Act: For the next seven days, add one gut-friendly food to your meals.

Start small and stay consistent.

Then notice how your digestion, mood and energy begin to shift.

72

Your Fork Can Beat Up Your Dumbbell

Abs are made in the kitchen. Unfortunately, so are gulab jamuns.

Let me save you five years and a few lakhs. I actually spent all this to learn this lesson. So, learn from my experience.

Between 2009 and 2014, I ran a chain of women's fitness centres. We sold 'fitness'. But what people wanted was 'fatness reduction'. Women came, sweated and lunged like warriors. But the weight just didn't budge.

One of our clients was Seema, a mother of two in her early thirties who never missed a workout. After exercising for three months, she didn't lose a single kilo. We were baffled. Until one day in the locker room, she laughed: 'Aaj toh 300 calories burn kiye … ab toh butter wala aloo paratha banta hai.'

There it was. She wasn't working out to lose fat. She was working out to earn food. The treadmill wasn't her fat burner. It had become her permission slip.

Your Plate > Your Push-ups

That's the day I learnt that exercise wasn't the hero. In fact, it was Circuit, the sidekick. The real Munnabhai was **diet**. That one plate of food has more power over your weight than an hour at the gym. Not fair? Maybe. But it's still true.

We finally said the one thing no gym owner wants to admit: weight loss is 80 per cent diet and 20 per cent exercise.[97] It took me five years of watching frustrated clients to finally admit this out loud.

No matter how hard we try, we can't outrun a bad diet. Depending on your run to erase your samosa is like using a Band-Aid on a fractured bone. It looks cute, but it's not very effective.

And average workout burns ~250 calories, while just one jalebi has ~450 calories.

It's like paying ₹500 off your credit card and then rewarding yourself by spending ₹1,000.

Where Exercise Actually Wins

Despite everything I've just said, it's not time to throw your sneakers out just yet. Exercise may not help you burn all the calories you've eaten, but it sure helps you:

- Build stamina and muscle
- Boost energy and mental health
- Delay ageing (so your knees don't start cracking in your forties)
- Assist in burning the *last* five stubborn kilos.

But the first 10 kilos? That's the job of your food.

Also, don't forget the importance of sleep. If you're sleeping less than six hours on a regular basis, stop expecting any kind of positive result from exercise or healthy food. Your sleep-deprived brain will crave junk and make sure you skip workouts. Sleep is the Wi-Fi of your metabolism. Without it, nothing connects properly.

Mic Drop: Real CEO, Please Stand Up

Food is the CEO of fat loss. Exercise is HR, and sleep the CFO. You don't get lean by working out harder. You do so by eating smarter, sleeping deeper and moving consistently. Most people get this triangle totally upside down. Let's flip it back.

Speaking of exercise, did you know most people do it all wrong? Let's fix that next.

73

You're Not Exercising—You're Just Walking and Talking

'Gym waale nahi haare bhaiya ... sofa jeet gaya.'

Let me confess something. Back when I ran a chain of fitness clubs, my biggest rival wasn't the gym across the street. It was the sofa. That perfect seat with the television set in front, a fridge nearby, the remote placed like it was installed by an ergonomics engineer. The sofa was a true masterpiece of passive resistance.

Around two-thirds of urban Indians don't exercise at all or do so rarely. And most of the rest walk in slow motion in parks. While talking about Modi, match results, marriage alliances and mango prices. They came for cardio and left with cholesterol and community gossip.

Why We Still Don't Move

We know exercise is good for us. It lowers stress, boosts our mood and increases our lifespan.

And our step count still competes with our screen time. And screen time's winning like it's on performance-enhancing drugs. Why? Because we either overcomplicate exercise like a start-up pitch deck or dismiss it like yet another 'Good Morning' forward.

Exercise is not just to lose weight. You do it so you can lift your suitcase without popping your spine. So you can dance at weddings without having to ice your knees the next morning. So you can live pain-free and not just look Instagram-ready.

Mistake #1: Walking Is Enough

Walking is good. But if you think just walking is enough for you, you're dead wrong.

For real fitness you need:

- *Strength* = Muscle + metabolism (squats, push-ups, resistance bands)
- *Cardio* = Heart + stamina (brisk walking, dancing, cycling, chasing cabs)
- *Flexibility* = Daily movement + injury prevention (yoga, stretches, touching your toes without crying)

Walking is only a third of your exercise goals. Would you pay ₹500 for chhole bhature … and be happy to be served just bhature?

Exactly.

Mistake #2: Walking = Fat Loss

I once met an uncle at a park in Siliguri. He proudly said, 'I've been walking every day for eight years!' I asked, 'Have you lost any weight?' 'I gained 20 kilos.' 'What's your walking speed?' 'Slow—like LIC paperwork.'

For fat-burning, you need to get your heart rate up. Here's the formula: **Max Heart Rate = 220 – your age.** So, if you're thirty, aim for 70 per cent of 190 = 133 beats per minute.

If you're walking slow enough to analyse Sharma-ji's daughter's qualities for marriage, your body is not in fat-burning mode. If you can gossip fluently while walking, you're basically strolling in a sari ad.

Excuses We All Use

Excuse 1: 'I don't have time.'

Sure. But last night, you watched twenty-seven reels of strangers eating pani puri in slow motion. Of course you have time. You're just spending it like a spoiled brat with a credit card.

Excuse 2: 'I can't go to the gym.'

That's all right. You don't need to. Bring the gym to your floor.

You already have the most powerful machine—your body.

Try this:

- Squats (for legs + glutes)
- Push-ups (for arms + chest)
- Planks (for core + quiet suffering)
- Lunges (for pride + pain)
- Crunches (every auntie's favourite to get abs magically)

Do this for about twenty minutes three to four times a week. That's enough to slow the ageing process. Add music and attitude to your exercise regimen, not excuses.

Mic Drop: Sitting Is the New Smoking

Sitting for more than ten hours a day increases the risk of cardiovascular-mortality by 62 per cent.[98] So, get up, stretch and walk right now. As soon as you have finished reading this sentence.

Your choice is simple: sweat for twenty minutes … or slowly become furniture. Because *gym waale nahi haare the*. That damn sofa just played dirty … and won.

Up next: How to build habits without any effort.

74

The One-Push-Up Secret

'He who does a little every day achieves more than one who waits for the perfect day.'

—Chanakya Niti (paraphrased)

'I can't follow any healthy habits for more than a week.'

A lot of people complain that they are unable to sustain healthy habits. They start their health habits with the energy of a Bollywood hero … and end them with the enthusiasm of a Monday morning alarm. Take solace in the fact that you're not alone.

So, how can you build a lifelong habit? And what should your first goal be?

An hour at the gym? Or a single push-up?

Most people would recommend the gym. But the smart ones—like Stephen Guise, author of *Mini Habits*—say the secret to change is starting ridiculously small. So small that it feels like cheating.

Motivation Dies. Habits Don't

Most people fail to form healthy habits because they treat health like a project. Something they'll 'do for a month'. But anything temporary gives temporary results. It's like applying moisturiser once and expecting supple skin for life.

Do you ever skip brushing your teeth? Probably not. Do you enjoy brushing your teeth? I doubt it. But you do it anyway—because it's a habit.

So if you want to change your life for the better, instead of chasing motivation, build habits.

From Nursery to Marathon

One of my teammates, RG from Gurgaon, wanted to run a marathon. He 'planned' to wake up at 5 a.m. every day, and run for two hours. There wasn't a day he woke up before 7 a.m. Here's how it went:

Me: What time do you actually wake up?

RG: 7.

Me: And you want to jump straight to a 5 a.m. run? That's not training. That's trauma.

RG: So what do I do?

Me: Wake up when you do every day and start with running for just ten minutes.

He laughed and said, 'That's too easy.' Exactly. That's why it works. Because your brain hates change and loves comfort. When you shock it, it rebels. But when you ease it in, the brain adapts.

Once you start running for ten minutes, you'll usually keep going. For much longer. But even on the worst days, doing that tiny bare minimum keeps the habit alive.

The Science of Stupidly Small

Picture a giant boulder at the edge of a cliff. You push, but it doesn't move. You keep pushing anyway. And finally, one nudge does the job and momentum takes over.

That's how habits work. Starting is the battle. Once you start, the rest flows easier. Small wins build trust with yourself. And trust builds transformation.

Everyone wants six-pack shortcuts. And it starts with one push-up.

Tiny Is Mighty

Discipline fails. Motivation dies. But habits stay and grow roots.

And one tiny habit, done daily, can rebuild your life faster than one giant goal you never start.

Up next: Systems > Goals

Do the Damn Thing: Shrink the Damn Goal

Reflect: What's one healthy action so small that you'd feel *silly* saying no to it?

Act: Pick your 'mini habit' today.

Try: One push-up, one glass of water after waking up, one fruit with lunch, a one-minute breathing break or one dance move while brushing your teeth.

Start small. Stay daily.

Your future self is watching. And slow-clapping for **you.**

75

Sexy Goals, Savage Systems

'You don't rise to the level of your goals. You fall to the level of your systems.'

—James Clear

Everyone loves goals. Lose weight, run a marathon, get six-pack abs before the next school reunion.

But here's the truth nobody wants to hear: goals don't get you to the finishing line. Systems do.

The Goal Trap (aka New Year's Hangover)

You know the drill:

- *'From tomorrow, I'll wake up at 5 a.m. and run 10 km.'*
- *'No sugar. Ever again.'*
- *'Gym every day. No excuses.'*

And by Day 3? Your alarm is muted. The laddoo calls your name. And your gym bag becomes an expensive dust collector.

While goals sound inspiring, motivation is that flaky friend who shows up late, talks big and ghosts you when it's go-time.

Systems, on the other hand, are boring. But they work every single time.

Goals Look Sexy. Systems Make Them Happen

Having a goal is like wanting to make biryani. A system is the recipe. Without it, you'll serve some bland rice and call it 'effort'.

Goal = Destination. System = Google Maps + fuel + snacks for the ride.

Let's say your goal is to lose 5 kg. But what's your system?

- Eat more protein.
- Sleep over seven hours.
- Strength train thrice a week.
- Limit oil to 4 tsp/day.
- Walk 8,000 steps.
- Stop eating like it's your last day on Earth.

It may sound boring, but boring wins championships.

Because momentum > motivation. Consistency > inspiration. Systems > vibes.

The Atomic Habits Shortcut

Thank you, James Clear, for giving us the Ikea manual for human behaviour.

Want to build good habits? The writer of *Atomic Habits* has a few suggestions.

- Make it obvious → Keep your shoes next to the bed. Fruit on the table.
- Make it attractive → Walk with music. Lift while blasting Bollywood bangers.
- Make it easy → 1 push-up is better than 0.
- Make it satisfying → Reward yourself with something that's not sugar.

Want to break bad ones?

- Make it invisible → Hide the chips. Log out of Zomato.
- Make it unattractive → Watch a video of what sugar does to your liver.
- Make it difficult → Add a screen time lock. Give your friend the password.
- Make it unsatisfying → Ask someone to roast you publicly when you screw up.

Burn the Motivation. Build the System

Motivation is mood-dependent. Systems are muscle memory. You don't want a fitness plan that only works on good days. You want one that still works when you're tired, heartbroken or just done with life.

Because success isn't a lightning bolt. It's a leaking tap. One day you'll look back and realise that you didn't hit your goal by magic. You just had a boring system that refused to quit.

And sometimes the key to the right systems is to have good company. Over to the next chapter.

Do the Damn Thing: System > Hype

Reflect: What's one habit you keep failing at because you're waiting to 'feel motivated'?

Act: Design a system so simple it can run on autopilot. Try:

- 10 squats after brushing
- 1 fruit with lunch
- No phone after 10 p.m.
- 1 glass of water before chai

Just small, daily wins are the real success strategy.

76

Stop Doing this Sh*t Alone

'Hang with chickens, you'll cluck. Hang with eagles, you'll fly.'
—*Steve Maraboli*

Trying to eat clean while your friends are inhaling cheese burst pizza is like quitting smoking at a hookah lounge. Your willpower doesn't stand a chance.

When people say no to alcohol, they're admired for their 'discipline'. But the moment they say no to dessert, they roll their eyes. '*Yaar, ek bite toh le.*' 'Bro, are you on a diet?' 'Come on, live a little!'

Junk food is the most socially accepted addiction in India. And it comes with peer pressure that's served hot with extra butter.

You Don't Just Need Motivation. You Need a Tribe

Your environment eats your willpower for breakfast. If everyone around you is digging into butter naan and gulab jamun, and you find it difficult to resist that, it's a war-like situation for you. But if your people are walking more, lifting weights, ordering grilled paneer, you've got momentum to meet your fitness goals.

Research says that people who pursue health goals together lose 24 per cent more weight than those who go solo.[99] So, it's time look for:

- A friend who celebrates your progress
- A partner who eats clean without drama
- A colleague who sends protein recipes instead of biryani reels
- And that one gym freak who drags you out even when you're dying inside (keep them forever).

But sometimes, even the best tribe isn't enough. That's when you need a coach.

Why You Still Don't Have Abs (Spoiler: YouTube Isn't Enough)

If books and YouTube were enough, every schoolkid would be a genius.

Every topper has a mentor. Every athlete has a coach. Every big glow-up has someone behind the scenes whispering, 'Don't quit today.'

We need mentors and coaches because they give us targets and how to reach them while also making sure we do so.

Coaches hold you accountable and stay when the going gets tough.

In the Mahabharata, Bhima—strong, proud, unstoppable—once found his path blocked by a monkey's tail. He scoffed: 'Move your tail, old monkey.' The monkey, who was Hanuman in disguise, said, 'You move it.' Bhima tried, but failed.

This shows us that how strong you are, someone wiser has walked the path before you. And real strength is knowing when to bow your head … and learn from them.

Abs Need Allies

None of us can succeed alone. Behind every six-pack is a team of protein shakes, pushy friends and one coach who refused to let you quit.

If you've failed at fitness before, maybe you weren't entirely to blame. Maybe you were just surrounded by the wrong voices. So, build your circle and find a mentor. Because while bodies are built in gyms, consistency is built in the community.

Want to see how ready your body (and mindset) really are? Grab a pen and flip to the Bonus Section. It's time to test your baseline.

Bonus: Your Health Audit

How Healthy Are Your Habits?

Instructions:
Rate each statement from 1 to 5
(1 = Never, 5 = Always)
Be honest, this is for your personal reflection.

1. Nutrition and Eating Habits

- ☐ I maintain a healthy weight.
- ☐ I don't see food as my enemy but a means to nourish my body.
- ☐ I include a protein source in every meal (aiming for at least 1 g per kg of body weight).
- ☐ I consume a variety of whole foods—fruits, vegetables, whole grains and legumes.
- ☐ I limit processed foods, refined carbs and excessive sugar.

2. Fats and Carbohydrates: Are You Choosing Right?

- [ ] I consume good fats (nuts, seeds, ghee, avocado) and avoid trans fats.
- [ ] I don't fear carbs but eat the right kind—whole grains over refined ones.
- [ ] I pair carbs with protein (for example, dal with rice) to slow sugar release.
- [ ] I consume enough fibre daily to aid digestion and gut health.
- [ ] I am mindful of my oil intake and use healthier cooking oils.

3. Exercise and Activity

- [ ] I exercise regularly (at least three to four times a week).
- [ ] I include strength training (bodyweight exercises, resistance training) in my routine.
- [ ] I walk at 70–75 per cent of my Maximum Heart Rate (MHR) instead of just strolling.
- [ ] I incorporate some stretching or mobility work to stay flexible.
- [ ] I avoid prolonged inactivity and try to stay active throughout the day.

4. Hydration and Gut Health

- [ ] I drink enough water daily to stay hydrated.
- [ ] I eat gut-friendly foods like fibre-rich vegetables, fermented foods or probiotics.
- [ ] I avoid overeating at night, which impacts digestion and metabolism.
- [ ] I practise Hara Hachi Bu (stopping at 80 per cent fullness instead of overeating).
- [ ] I eat slowly and mindfully instead of rushing through meals.

5. Healthy Habits and Lifestyle

- ☐ I avoid extreme crash diets and focus on long-term sustainable nutrition.
- ☐ I don't let one unhealthy meal derail my progress; I get back on track.
- ☐ I believe that systems are more important than willpower.
- ☐ I realise that consistency is more important than intensity, and I follow my healthy habits consistently.
- ☐ I see health as an investment, not a sacrifice, and make conscious choices.

Your Score and Reflection

90+ points: Excellent! You're on track for great health.

70–89 points: You're doing well, but some areas need attention.

50–69 points: Time to level up! Focus on two to three key improvements.

Below 50 points: Start small but start today! One habit at a time.

Final Thought:

Your body is your real home—take care of it like you would a your car. Small changes lead to lifelong health!

Before You Go: The Story Beneath Every Story

'It is a good divine that follows his own instructions.'
—William Shakespeare

If you've made it this far, thank you. Not just for turning the pages, but for staying through the laughs, heartbreaks, uncomfortable truths and awkward metaphors.

Before you shut this book, I want to tell you where it really began.

The Boy Who Couldn't Say 'Hello'

I grew up a quiet kid in a small town called Katihar in Bihar in a middle-class family. Until Class V, my English vocabulary was basically just the alphabet song. I'd stare at a sentence for twenty minutes and still not know what it meant.

Later, when I moved to Darjeeling and Siliguri, my small-town accent became a joke. When people laughed at it, I froze. I had plenty to say, but felt that silence was safer than shame.

There was a time I couldn't even say 'Hello' on the phone without rehearsing it. I felt invisible. And there were days I wondered if the world would be better off without me.

The Day Everything Changed

In Class XI, I made it to the science stream at DPS R.K. Puram. Getting admission to that prestigious school in Delhi was a dream for half the country then. But I felt hollow. I'm sure I'd have felt the same if I'd cracked IIT. I didn't believe in myself, so what was the point of any sort of achievement when I didn't even like the person in the mirror.

On Day 1 at my new school, I did something wild: I quit the science stream and chose commerce. On Day 1 at my new school, I did something wild: I quit the science stream and chose commerce. I wanted to become a better human being before becoming a 'professional'. Commerce gave me the space to work on myself.

In 1999, I picked up *You Can Win* by Shiv Khera. I read through every page several times and his words cracked open something in me. Since then, I've devoured hundreds of books, attended workshops, asked scary questions and started piecing myself back together.

Why I Wrote This

Writing books are a vanity project for some people. But I just wanted to pass on everything I've learnt so far with my book. We've all been broken somewhere. It could be confidence, in our career and relationships, or health-wise. The cracks are different, but the silence is the same.

At such moments, we have two choices: wait for life to break us before we learn, or learn from someone who's already been broken … and rebuilt their life.

This book is my way of saying: 'You're not alone.' If even one chapter made you feel a little stronger, a little lighter, a little more seen, then every word was worth it.

The Final Mic Drop

Write your top learnings.

The Final 'Do the Damn Thing'

What have you implemented from the book?

Change happens with change.

If this book helped you, pass the light. Someone else is still walking in the dark.

Notes

1 'World Happiness Report 2025', *Sustainable Development Solutions Network*, March 2025, https://worldhappiness.report.

2 Albert Ellis, *A Guide to Rational Living*, Wilshire Book Co., 1975.

3 Tony Robbins, *Awaken the Giant Within*, Simon & Schuster, 1991.

4 'Mental Health and Emotion Regulation in Indian Youth', Indian Institute of Management Bangalore, Department of Behavioural Sciences, 2021, https://iimb.ac.in/research/mental-health-youth.

5 Shefali Tsabary, *A Radical Awakening: Turn Pain into Power, Embrace Your Truth, Live Free*, HarperCollins India, 2021.

6 Sheryl Sandberg and Adam Grant, *Option B: Facing Adversity, Building Resilience, and Finding Joy*, Penguin Random House, 2017.

7 Eknath Easwaran (trans.), *The Bhagavad Gita*, Nilgiri Press, 1985.

8 *National Mental Health Survey of India 2019–2022*, National Institute of Mental Health and Neurosciences (NIMHANS), 2023, https://nimhans.ac.in.

9 'Cognitive Behavioral Therapy Enhances Brain Circuits to Relieve Depression', Stanford Medicine News Center, 6 September 2024, https://med.stanford.edu/news/all-news/2024/09/cognitive-behaviora-therapy-depression.html.

10 'Giving Thanks Can Make You Happier', Harvard Health Publishing, 14 August 2021, https://www.health.harvard.edu/healthbeat/giving-thanks-can-make-you-happier.

11 Nick Vujicic, *Life Without Limits: Inspiration for a Ridiculously Good Life*, WaterBrook Press, 2010.

12 Robert A. Emmons and Michael E. McCullough, 'Counting Blessings Versus Burdens: An Experimental Investigation of Gratitude and Subjective Well-Being', *Journal of Personality and Social Psychology*, 84 (2): 377–389, 2003.

13 Patanjali, *Yoga Sutra 2.42 — Santosha (Contentment)*, transl. Eknath Easwaran, Nilgiri Press, 1985.

14 Malala Yousafzai and Christina Lamb, *I Am Malala: The Girl Who Stood Up for Education and Was Shot by the Taliban*, Little, Brown and Company, 2013.

15 Sri Sri Ravi Shankar, *Celebrating Silence*, Jaico Publishing House, 2002.

16 Loren L. Toussaint, Everett L. Worthington Jr., and David R. Williams, 'Forgiveness, Stress, and Health: A Review and Theoretical Framework', *Journal of Behavioral Medicine*, 34(6): 484–495, 2011.

17 'NASA, Earth Facts: Rotation and Orbit', *NASA Space Science Data Portal*, 2024, https://nssdc.gsfc.nasa.gov/planetary/factsheet/earthfact.html.

18 Eknath Easwaran (trans.), *The Bhagavad Gita*, The Nilgiri Press, 1985.

19 Michael A. Singer, *The Surrender Experiment: My Journey into Life's Perfection*, Harmony, 2015.

20 Arunima Sinha, *Born Again on the Mountain: A Story of Losing Everything and Finding It Back*, Penguin India, 2014.

21 Yuval Noah Harari, *Sapiens: A Brief History of Humankind*, Harper, 2015.

22 'Chronic Complaining Can Shrink the Hippocampus', *Stanford Medicine Blog*, 10 April 2019, https://med.stanford.edu/blog/chronic-complaining.html.

23 Tim Ferriss, *The 4-Hour Workweek*, Crown, 2007.

24 'Stress Relief from Laughter: It's No Joke', *Mayo Clinic Health System*, 2023, https://www.mayoclinic.org/healthy-lifestyle/stress-management/in-depth/stress-relief/art-20044456.

25 'Physical Activity and Health', WHO Factsheet, 2023, *World Health Organization*, https://www.who.int/news-room/fact-sheets/detail/physical-activity.

26 *Harvard Study of Adult Development, 1938–2023*, Harvard University, https://adultdevelopmentstudy.org.

27 'World Happiness Report 2024', Sustainable Development Solutions Network, March 2024, https://worldhappiness.report.

28 C. Rajagopalachari (transl.), *Mahabharata (Yaksha Prashna)*, Bharatiya Vidya Bhavan, 1951.

29 Robert Waldinger and Marc Schulz, *The Good Life: Lessons from the World's Longest Scientific Study of Happiness*, Simon & Schuster, 2023.
30 *Indian Youth and Work Survey 2023*, Pew Research Center, November 2023.
31 Julianne Holt-Lunstad, Timothy B. Smith, and J. Bradley Layton, 'Loneliness and Social Isolation as Risk Factors for Mortality: A Meta-Analytic Review', *Perspectives on Psychological Science*, 10(2): 227–237, 2015.
32 Hector García and Francesc Miralles, *Ikigai: The Japanese Secret to a Long and Happy Life*, Penguin Life, 2017.
33 'The Future of Recruiting Report 2023 (India Edition)', LinkedIn India, January 2023, https://business.linkedin.com/content/dam/me/business/en-in/talent-solutions/resources/pdfs/future-of-recruiting-report-2023.pdf.
34 Gail Matthews, 'The Impact of Commitment, Accountability, and Written Goals on Goal Achievement', Dominican University of California, 2007.
35 Tyna Eloundou, Sam Manning, Pamela Mishkin and Daniel Rock, 'GPTs are GPTs: An Early Look at the Labor Market Impact Potential of Large Language Models', *Cornell University*, 2023, arXiv:2303.10130.
36 Carol S. Dweck, *Mindset: The New Psychology of Success*, Random House, 2006.
37 Norman Doidge, *The Brain that Changes Itself*, Viking Penguin, 2007.
38 Julian B. Rotter, 'Generalized Expectancies for Internal versus External Control of Reinforcement', *Psychological Monographs*, 80(1): 1–28, 1966.
39 Yuval Noah Harari, *Sapiens: A Brief History of Humankind*, Harper, 2015.
40 Chris Bailey, 'A Foolproof Way to Get Up Early Every Morning', ChrisBailey.com, 3 December 2021.
41 Thomas C. Corley, *Rich Habits: The Daily Success Habits of Wealthy Individuals*, Templeton Press, 2010.
42 A.P. Hill and T. Curran, 'Multidimensional Perfectionism and Burnout: A Meta-Analysis', *Personality & Social Psychology Review*, 20(3), 2016, 269-288.
43 Malcolm Gladwell, *Blink: The Power of Thinking Without Thinking*, Little, Brown, 2005.
44 G.S. Adams, B.A. Converse, A.H. Hales and L.E. Klotz, 'People systematically overlook subtractive changes', *Nature*, 592, 2021, 258–261, https://doi.org/10.1038/s41586-021-03380-y.

45 'Work Trend Index: Will AI Fix Work?' *Microsoft WorkLab*, 9 May 2023, https://www.microsoft.com/en-us/worklab/work-trend-index/will-ai-fix-work.
46 Cal Newport, *Deep Work*, Grand Central, 2016.
47 Naval Ravikant, *The Almanack of Naval Ravikant*, ed. Eric Jorgenson, Tim Ferriss Publishing, 2020.
48 'How Many Applicants Per Job? (2023 Data)', Zippia.com, 2023.
49 Antoine Bechara, et al. 'A Neural Basis for Decision-Making and the Role of Emotion in the Iowa Gambling Task', *Science*, 275(5304), 1997, 1293–1295.
50 Malcolm Gladwell, *Blink: The Power of Thinking Without Thinking*, Little, Brown, 2005.
51 Nataliya Kosmyna, Eugene Hauptmann, Ye Tong Yuan, Jessica Situ, Xian-Hao Liao, Ashly Vivian Beresnitzky, Iris Braunstein and Pattie Maes, 'Your Brain on ChatGPT: Accumulation of Cognitive Debt when Using an AI Assistant for Essay Writing Task', 10 June 2025, arXiv preprint arXiv:2506.08872.
52 'National Strategy for Financial Education 2020–2025', Reserve Bank of India, RBI/2020-21/66.
53 'Personal Finance Literacy Survey 2023', Zerodha, 2023.
54 'Fantasy Sports User Base Crosses 130 Million: Dream11 Leads Growth', *The Economic Times, ET Bureau*, 2023.
55 'Lottery Winner Jack Whittaker Says "I Wish I'd Torn That Ticket Up"', *ABC News*, 6 April 2007, https://abcnews.go.com/Entertainment/story?id=3001385&page=1.
56 'How India Gives 2020-21: Household Giving Survey', Kantar Worldpanel & Ashoka University, September 2022.
57 'Millionaire Outlook Study', Fidelity Investments, Fidelity, 2017.
58 'Periodic Labour Force Survey (PLFS) 2022–23', Government of India.
59 'Elon Musk's child seeks name change, citing gender identity and relationship with father', *Reuters*, 21 June 2022.
60 Eamonn Forde, 'Death & taxes: The Michael Jackson estate, the IRS and posthumous celebrity valuations', *Forbes*, 4 May 2021, https://www.forbes.com/sites/eamonnforde/2021/05/04/death--taxes-the-michael-jackson-estate-the-irs-and-posthumous-celebrity-valuations/.
61 Morgan Housel, 'The Man in the Car Paradox', *The Psychology of Money*, Harriman House, 2020.
62 'Annual Report 2022', Chairman's Letter, Berkshire Hathaway Inc.
63 Gregory Zuckerman, *The Man Who Solved the Market: How Jim Simons Launched the Quant Revolution*, Penguin Portfolio, 2019.

64 H. Bessembinder, 'Do stocks outperform Treasury bills? (Working Paper No. 17-56)', W. P. Carey School of Business, Arizona State University, November 2017, https://papers.ssrn.com/sol3/papers.cfm?abstract_id=2900447.

65 'Gross savings (% of GDP) – India (Indicator: NY.GDS.TOTL.ZS)', World Bank, 2024, https://data.worldbank.org/indicator/NY.GDS.TOTL.ZS?locations=IN.

66 E.W. Dunn, D.T. Gilbert and T.D. Wilson, 'Everyday drug: When making decisions, people underestimate the full experience of adaptation', *Journal of Consumer Psychology*, 21(2), 2011, 115-125, https://doi.org/10.1016/j.jcps.2011.02.002.

67 Naomi I. Eisenberger, Matthew D. Lieberman and Kipling D. Williams, 'Does Rejection Hurt? An fMRI Study of Social Exclusion', *Science*, 302(5643), 2003, 290–292.

68 Diana I. Tamir and Jason P. Mitchell, 'Disclosing information about the self is intrinsically rewarding', *Proceedings of the National Academy of Sciences (PNAS)*, 2012.

69 Brian L. Mishara and Normand B. Martin, 'Effects of Telephone Intervention for Suicide Prevention', *Suicide and Life-Threatening Behavior*, 2012.

70 Raymond S. Nickerson, 'Confirmation Bias: A Ubiquitous Phenomenon in Many Guises', *Review of General Psychology*, 1998.

71 Deborah Tannen, *You Just Don't Understand: Women and Men in Conversation*, Ballantine Books, 1990.

72 Shelley E. Taylor, 'Biobehavioral responses to stress in females: Tend-and-befriend, not fight-or-flight', *Psychological Review*, 2000.

73 Terri D. Fisher, Zachary T. Moore and Mary-Jo Pittenger, 'Sex on the Brain? An Examination of Frequency of Sexual Cognitions as a Function of Gender, Erotophilia, and Social Desirability', *Journal of Sex Research*, 49(1), 2012, 69–77.

74 Peter B. Gray and Justin R. Garcia, *Evolution and Human Sexual Behavior*, Harvard University Press, 2013.

75 Eli J. Finkel, Jeffry A. Simpson and Paul W. Eastwick, 'The Psychology of Close Relationships: Fourteen Core Principles', *Annual Review of Psychology*, 2017.

76 Christopher D. Fiorillo, Philippe N. Tobler and Wolfram Schultz, 'Distributions of Reward Probability and Uncertainty in Dopamine Neurons', *Science*, 299(5614): 1898–1902, 2003.

77 John M. Gottman and Nan Silver, *The Seven Principles for Making Marriage Work*, Harmony Books, 2015.

78 'Why Childhood Trauma Affects Adult Relationships', *American Psychological Association*, 2023.

79 Sigmund Freud, *Beyond the Pleasure Principle*, International Psycho-Analytical Library, 1920.

80 F. J. Charlson et al., 'Mental disorders among adults in India: prevalence and risk factors', *Lancet Psychiatry*, 2021.

81 *Diagnostic and Statistical Manual of Mental Disorders* (5th ed.), American Psychiatric Association, 2013.

82 Daniel Kahneman and Amos Tversky, 'Prospect Theory: An Analysis of Decision Under Risk', *Econometrica 47*, no. 2, 1979, 263–291.

83 'History of the Coca-Cola Santa Claus', Coca-Cola Company, 2023.

84 S. Bassi, V. Gupta and J. Kishore, 'Content analysis of food advertisements on popular Indian television channels among children and youth: A cross-sectional study', *Journal of Global Health Reports*, 2021.

85 J.C.G. Halford et al., 'Effect of television advertisements for foods on food consumption in children', *Appetite*, 2004.

86 J. Polivy and C.P. Herman, 'The Effects of Restraint on Food Intake: Forbidden Fruit or Undieting?', *International Journal of Eating Disorders*, 38(4), 2005, 307–312, https://doi.org/10.1002/eat.20195.

87 M. Sharma, A. Kishore and D. Roy, 'Indian diets and the EAT-Lancet recommendations: A gap analysis', *Global Food Security*, 26, 2020, 100415.

88 T. Ohkuma, Y. Hirakawa, U. Nakamura, Y. Kiyohara, T. Kitazono and T. Ojima, 'Association between eating rate and obesity: A systematic review and meta-analysis', *International Journal of Obesity*, 39(11), 2015, 1589–1596.

89 C.P. Herman and D. Mack, 'Restrained and unrestrained eating', *Journal of Personality*, 43(4), 1975.

90 Shoba Suri, 'India's Protein Deficiency and the Need to Address the Problem', *Observer Research Foundation*, 2020.

91 M. Lonnie, 'Protein for Life: Review of optimal protein intake, sustainable diets and the influence of exercise and ageing', *Nutrients*, 10(10), 2018, https://doi.org/10.3390/nu10101306.

92 D.S. Weigle et al., 'A high-protein diet induces sustained reductions in appetite, ad libitum caloric intake and body weight', *American Journal of Clinical Nutrition*, 82(1), 2005, 41-48.

93 J.S. O'Brien and E.L. Sampson, 'Lipid composition of the normal human brain', *Journal of Lipid Research*, 6(4), 1965, 537–544.

94 Michael D. Gershon, *The Second Brain: A Groundbreaking New Understanding of Nervous Disorders of the Stomach and Intestine*, HarperCollins, 1998.

95 Vanessa K. Ridaura et al., 'Gut Microbiota from Twins Discordant for Obesity Modulate Metabolism in Mice', *Science*, 341(6150), 2013.

96 John R. Kelly et al., 'Transferring the Blues: Depression-Associated Gut Microbiota Induces Neurobehavioural Changes in Rats', *Journal of Psychiatric Research*, 82, 2016.

97 Kevin D. Hall et al., 'Energy Balance and Its Components: Implications for Body Weight Regulation', *The American Journal of Clinical Nutrition*, 95(4), 2012, 989–994.

98 L. F. M. Rezende, M. Ahmadi, G. Ferrari et al., 'Device-measured sedentary time and intensity-specific physical activity in relation to all-cause and cardiovascular disease mortality: the UK Biobank cohort study', *International Journal of Behavioral Nutrition and Physical Activity*, 21:68, 2024.

99 D.A. Renjilian, M.G. Perri, M.C. Limacher, P.E. Durning, A.D. Martin and D. Lithgow, 'Enhancing weight loss maintenance in obese patients: The role of group cohesion', *International Journal of Obesity*, 25(7), 2001, 1036–1041.